Bankim Chandra Chattopadhyay

# Bankim Chandra Chattopadhyay

## An Intellectual Biography

Amiya P. Sen

OXFORD
UNIVERSITY PRESS

**OXFORD**
UNIVERSITY PRESS

YMCA Library Building, Jai Singh Road, New Delhi 110 001

Oxford University Press is a department of the University of Oxford. It furthers the University's objective of excellence in research, scholarship, and education by publishing worldwide in

Oxford New York
Auckland Cape Town Dar es Salaam Hong Kong Karachi
Kuala Lumpur Madrid Melbourne Mexico City Nairobi
New Delhi Shanghai Taipei Toronto

With offices in
Argentina Austria Brazil Chile Czech Republic France Greece
Guatemala Hungary Italy Japan Poland Portugal Singapore
South Korea Switzerland Thailand Turkey Ukraine Vietnam

Oxford is a registered trademark of Oxford University Press in the UK and in certain other countries

Published in India
by Oxford University Press, New Delhi



First published 2008



ISBN 13: 978-0-19-569503-8
ISBN 10: 0-19-569503-8

Typeset in ITC Espirit 10.5/12.8
by Sai Graphic Design, New Delhi 110 055
Printed in India at Rajshri Photolithographers, Delhi 110 032
Published by Oxford University Press
YMCA Library Building, Jai Singh Road, New Delhi 110 001

*For the two Sujatas [Varma and Nag], Anil, Shikha, Rana, Tomji, Sherina, Savita, Elizabeth, Kumkum, Malabika, and Keya—friends who have been most indulgent and kind over the years*

# General Editor's Note

This book is part of a series of short biographies of men and women from the late nineteenth century to the present day, who have contributed in discrete ways towards building modern India. With a non-specialist readership in mind, the biographies will provide concise, authoritative introductions to the lives and works of individuals who have had the courage to pursue their own visions and vocations—in the process, often touching the lives of many others in a positive and substantial way. These stories of outstanding lives seek to understand and appreciate achievements rather than provide a straightforward chronological retelling. We hope the biographies succeed in recapturing the topography of the past without hagiography and nostalgia.

NARAYANI GUPTA

# *Contents*

# *Preface*

This biography was written through the scorching summer of 2007, at a time when friends and colleagues had wisely taken to other pursuits. It is a work that I have wanted to write for a long time but could not, for lack of either time or courage. Over the years, it has increasingly occurred to me that writing on Bankim was no easy matter, more so for a historian with only a superficial understanding of literary refinements and abstract philosophical questions. Lucidly summarizing works like Bankim's *Dharmatattwa* or *Krishna Charitra* proved exasperatingly difficult at times. On the other hand, I have all along been driven by the belief that this is a biography that I owe as much to Bankim as to myself for the way his writings have sustained my interest in modern Hinduism and the self-reflexivity of modern Hindus. This is an obligation I am happy at having fulfilled.

This is the second time that Oxford University Press has graciously invited me to contribute and keep alive the 'Modern Indian Greats' series. My first contribution to the series, as some might recall, was a biography of Swami Vivekananda, which, I am happy to note, has gained more fame than notoriety. I would like to thank Oxford University Press, New Delhi, and Professor Narayani Gupta (Narayanidi to me), General Editor of the series, for encouraging me with this project. Thanks also go to Simi Malhotra, friend and colleague, for painstakingly going through the typescript. This would be an apt occasion to remind them all of how grateful I am for their constructive criticism and of the personal satisfaction I have had writing for them.

Unless otherwise stated, all translations from the Bengali originals used in this work are mine. I have also included two appendices in the hope that these would be of some interest to the general reader.

New Delhi
*Rath Yatra*, 2007

AMIYA P. SEN

# 1

# *Situating Bankim Chandra*

No nation can grow without finding a fit and satisfying medium of expression for the new self into which it was developing—without a language which shall give permanent shape to its thoughts and feelings and carry every new impulse swiftly and triumphantly into the consciousness of all. It was Bankim's first great service to India that he gave the race which stood in its vanguard such a perfect and satisfying medium.

—Sri Aurobindo (1907)

In an essay written for the Bengali daily, *Ananda Bazar Patrika* in 1998, Nirad C. Chaudhuri ranked Bankim Chandra Chattopadhyay as the greatest Bengali after Rabindranath Tagore. Together with Tagore, he was identified with much that characterized modern Bengalis—their private sentiments, intellectual interests, and aesthetic preferences. Predictably, Chaudhuri's essay brought forth a number of contesting claims, based as these were on differing perceptions of what constitutes greatness or just how these might be measured. The persuasiveness of Chaudhuri's arguments, as one recalls, rested on a sharp separation of history and hagiography. Pre-modern hagiographies, as Chaudhuri had argued, associated greatness with miraculous and superhuman feats. On the contrary, modern Western-educated Bengalis measured this in very human terms.

In the context of Bankim Chandra's life and work, this is indeed an important statement to make, for here, human character was seen to emerge from a sense of engagement with the world. First, there was the acknowledgement of one's duties towards the community and thereafter, a selfless effort at meeting these. Inasmuch as he accepted the idea of God's recurring descent on earth as an avatar, Bankim did tend to read history in terms of some divinely ordained scheme. On the other hand, his magnum opus, *Krishna Charitra* (1886) also asserts that when He descended on earth, even God was constrained to act fully like a man. As an avatar, God sought the solution to pressing human problems through rational acts, employing powers of the human body and mind.

It is also apt that a man like Bankim be judged in very contemporary terms for though his life and work negotiated with both modernity and tradition and sought relevance in both, the overarching purpose was to contemporize the past rather than locate the modern in some remote antiquity. Bankim Chandra consistently rejected the Vedic revival of Pandit Dayanand Saraswati (1824–83) on the grounds that this was archaic, irrational, and ill-equipped to meet modern needs. This was also the intention behind his attempt to re-interpret the Bhagavad Gita, brushing aside commentaries offered by older and more revered commentators. In assessing Bankim therefore, one must pay as much attention to the question of substance as to form; to what he said as much as to the language in which he chose to communicate his intentions. Scholars rightly stress Bankim's lasting contribution to modern Bengali prose and to new literary forms like the novel, but tend to overlook the possibility that this may have been tied to a larger purpose. Perhaps it is the urge to say new things that led Bankim Chandra to literary and linguistic experimentations. By comparison, other Bengali authors like Peary Chand Mitra (1814–83) and Iswar Chandra Vidyasagar (1820–91) whose prose he tried to improve upon, had little to say that was new.

Historically, the most productive phase of Bankim's life and career coincided with the high noon of the 'Bengal Renaissance' as also with its palpable weakening. The mental and moral revolutions that characterized upper-caste, educated Bengalis by the second half of the nineteenth century were creatively manifested in Bankim Chandra, and yet, ironically, he was among those who witnessed a backtracking in respect of some of its cherished values. At the time of his graduation, Bankim could wholeheartedly accept the idea of British rule leading India to the path of modernity and progress. Some years later, he was to lament how even after ruling the country for over a hundred years, the British had failed to truly comprehend India and the Indians.

In his essay, Nirad C. Chaudhuri also draws our attention to the rather polarized perceptions on Bankim Chandra. To an extent, this reflects the many conflicting sides to the man himself. In his day, he was under attack from various quarters ranging from orthodox Sanskritists who disapproved of his linguistic innovations to Christian missionaries who accused him of siding with idolatry and superstition. Bankim befriended some of his English superiors but bravely confronted those whom he knew to be in the wrong. Colonial officials suspected him of harbouring disloyalty and, in all probability, this also explains why his professional experience and competence were not suitably rewarded. Testimonies and personal accounts left behind by his close friends and admirers often speak of the complex dimensions to Bankim's character. Some found him to be short-tempered and unsociable, others, conceited but courageous. To some, he was an extremely gifted individual but morally inconsistent, while others found him to be rather self-opinionated and unwilling to acknowledge talent in friends and fellow writers.

It has even been suggested that Bankim knew very little of contemporary Bengali literature and never hesitated to express his feelings even if these were against prevailing public sentiments. An apt example here is his conception of Krishna in his *Krishna Charitra*, which ran counter to the god as conceived in both high textual culture and popular devotion. And though he was much acclaimed for his contribution to nation-building, not everybody initially agreed with his conception of the nation and nationalism. Here it would be interesting to note that neither the patriotic novel *Anandamath* (1882) nor the evocative song 'Vande Mataram' that it included, attained any degree of popularity in Bankim's lifetime. On the contrary, even his close friends thought that the plot of the novel was rather contrived and that the characters he had created better fitted European ideals rather than Indian ones. Especially after his death, he was also accused of fanning communal sentiments, again largely through his historical novels wherein allegedly, the Hindu had been highly praised and the Muslim unduly vilified. There are, however, critics who argue that Bankim's real intention was to expose human weaknesses and follies and here evidently, he made no distinction between the Hindu and the Muslim. Finally, there still rages some controversy on whether in his thought and expression, Bankim Chandra was more of a 'revivalist' than a 'reformer'. Some saw in him a thinker who unduly wished to revive older social and cultural forms while others accused him of so radically changing the face of Hinduism that it could hardly be recognized. In a sense, this is a vacuous debate for within the cultural framework of neo-Hinduism, revival always implied a degree of reform, and reform often appeared to be an attempt to revive the 'authentic' religious and cultural life of the Hindus. The life and work of Bankim Chandra reminds us of the need to separate the conservative Hindu from the reactionary, a critical approach to the past from its thoughtless replication, and a creative acceptance of cross-cultural influences from the blind rejection of all 'alien' influences.

Although he is now a well-known author whose major works are read in several Indian and non-Indian languages, there is still a case for understanding Bankim as an essentially provincial figure who chose to write for a specific community—the Western-educated, middle classes in Bengal. In the song 'Vande Mataram', it is Bengal (albeit in a larger territorial sense) that is perceived as the Mother, not India as a whole. The fact that he rarely travelled beyond Bengal, not to speak of India, does tend to separate him from some of his well-known contemporaries or near-contemporaries like Raja Rammohun Roy (1774–1833), Keshub Chandra Sen (1838–84), and Swami Vivekananda (1863–1902), all of whom took their cultural and religious missions to the West. Bankim's fame as an interpreter of his tradition therefore does not rest on what has been aptly described as the 'pizza effect'. Thanks to what Italian emigrants to the United States did with it, the pizza was progressively transformed from a coarse bread to its currently known form, and successfully re-introduced into its country of origin. Something similar seems to have occurred with Hindu religion and culture in modern times, especially in the hands of those who exposed these to the Western gaze. Bankim's own agenda, on the contrary, was distinctly counter-Orientalist. We do not detect here the double problematic of having to win over both the Western intelligentsia and the educated middle classes back home. Effectively, he chose to focus on the latter, guided by the belief that the project of building a new India required empathy, understanding, and moral responsibility that this class alone could produce.

## A Province in Transition, A People in Transition

After the Battle of Plassey (1757), the political revolution in Bengal proceeded briskly, bringing with it a rapid succession of changes. This stands in some contrast to developments in Sind or the Punjab where British rule arrived later and Western values were relatively slower to take root. That Bengal was subjugated early and remained, for some length of time, the nucleus of British power in India was to have important consequences for its people. Educated, upper-class Bengalis were the first to be exposed to new ideologies and methods of ordering their daily lives, and an intellectual and social transformation followed in the wake of such influences. On the other hand, a reaction to such changes was also quick to set in. The rapidity and manner in which the colonial transformation was effected in Bengal would explain why over time, Bengalis, and more specifically Bengali Hindus, turned out to be not only great admirers of British rule but also its earliest critics.

The political revolution in Bengal was accompanied by significant changes in the local economy and society. To an extent, of course, such changes subtly combined with certain continuities and long-term trends. Thus, like the preceding Mughal state, the colonial state too tried to maximize revenue extraction from the land. For the early colonial state, an assured and copious revenue from land was necessary on two counts. First, it allowed traders of the East India Company (hereafter, the Company) to pay for their purchases in India with resources generated within the country itself. In British mercantilist thinking, this constituted a check on the outflow of precious bullion from the home country (Britain). Income generated from the land, sometimes through sheer extortion and plunder, also allowed the Company to meet its growing military expenditure at the time. Sadly, these compulsions blinded the Company to changing conditions in the Indian countryside. In its early days, even natural catastrophes would not get the Company to lower its revenue demand. Thus, notwithstanding the devastating famine that affected north Bengal in 1769–70, the Company's administration is known to have collected nearly as much revenue in the following year (1771–2) as it did during the year preceding the famine. This human tragedy forms the backdrop of Bankim's well-known novel *Anandamath.* Horrifying stories of how starving peasants were forced to feed on field rats while British revenue collectors went about exacting their dues gained wide currency in eighteenth century Bengal, and became a part of public memory. Bankim heard such stories from an extremely old relative who might have been born sometime in the 1760s, but he also personally witnessed similar conditions that recurred during the Orissa famine of 1866. It may not be fortuitous after all that he and an older brother, Sanjib Chandra, were inspired to comment at length on the plight of the Bengal peasantry.

It is also true, however, that over time, investment in land became attractive, especially in and around Calcutta. Earnings made in state service or through usury and collaborative trade were now used for buying estates. In early colonial Bengal, this was true of two prominent families, those of Rammohun Roy, and of his friend, Dwarkanath Tagore. Modest investments in land were also made by relatively better placed Hindu middle class households. By the third quarter of the nineteenth century, rent-incomes from estates constituted an extra source of income for middle class service-holders in Calcutta, though rising food prices and the fragmentation of already modest holdings were to substantially erode the economic value of such incomes. Sub-infeudation was anyway a growing habit with new investors, with many of them preferring to live in Calcutta and mofussil towns.

By one estimate, there were over 1.5 lakh estates of varying sizes by 1872–3.

By the second quarter of the nineteenth century, several important developments had come to be associated with the colonial city of Calcutta. First, there was its rapid emergence as the seat of political power. After 1772, government establishments were shifted out of Murshidabad, once the capital of the Bengal Nawabs, to this new colonial city. This at once led to the exodus of a large number of old service holders and business professionals who were now ready to switch loyalties. The other easily noticeable feature was Calcutta's rapid growth as a centre of booming overseas trade. Many more ships were anchored at Calcutta than at the older commercial port of Hoogly patronized by the Nawabs. Brisk trade was carried out in sugar, silk, cotton cloth, and indigo, and the profits of this trade were invested in what came to be known as Agency Houses. By 1803, almost thirty of these Houses had sprung up in the vicinity of Calcutta. Besides managing savings, these Houses were also known to finance long-distance shipping.

This trade, it must be noted, was marked by a high degree of Indo-European collaboration. As Europeans were at the time barred from holding land in their names, they were forced to operate through their Indian friends and business partners. The English trade in indigo, for example, was dependent on Indian producers and middlemen, and over time, this went on to create a class of merchants, shippers, and financiers whose economic interests were closely tied with one another. After 1813, when the Company lost its monopoly over the India trade, there was a greater influx of Europeans to Bengal, and consequently, a greater degree of commercial penetration of the province. Some prominent Bengalis, intimately connected with usury and trade, openly welcomed such changes. In 1833, when the Company's Charter came up for renewal before the British Parliament, Dwarkanath Tagore, the grandfather of the poet Rabindranath, spoke at public meetings, trying to draw attention to the pecuniary advantages that both Bengali landlords and peasant producers were apparently deriving from the indigo trade. Both Dwarkanath and his close friend, Rammohun Roy, were on the side of 'Free Traders', and believed that greater European colonization of India would lead to substantial, all-round progress. Sadly, such hopes proved to be greatly misplaced for, even by the 1830s, the nature or pattern of Indo-British trade had begun to appreciably change, and in a manner that was clearly to the disadvantage of Indians. Even as early as 1800, Bengal muslin, hitherto a principal item of export from India, was under some threat from British competition. Every effort was now made to discourage the export of Indian cottons to the British market. Thus, import duties on Indian cottons were upwardly revised nine times during the period 1802–19. On the other hand, cotton yarns imported from England were forced upon Dacca weavers by 1824. This led to the systematic destruction of the Indian handloom industry, especially at centres producing fine cottons. Indian weavers were henceforth increasingly reduced to the status of full-time servants of the Company and were forced to work on unremunerative wages.

Calcutta, even by the 1820s, had grown to be a fairly populous city. By one estimate, its population in the year 1822 was over 2,00,000 to which were daily added a good number of migrants arriving from the neighbouring areas in search of opportunities and employment. These people worked in various capacities—as clerks, coolies, traders, translators, students, and private tutors. On the other hand, by 1823, Bishop Heber (later the Lord Bishop of Calcutta), who briefly camped in this city, could already spot its many paradoxes. He described the European part of the city as 'a very noble city with tall and stately buildings', whereas in the Indian quarters what greeted him were 'deep, bleak and dingy, narrow crooked streets, huts of earth baked in the sun … interspersed here and there with ruinous brick bazaars (and) pools of dirty water'. However, it was not simply the prospect of material gain that attracted people to Calcutta; the city was now also seen as a place where people might want to settle down and pursue a wide range of interests. The apt example of this is that of Rammohun himself, whose emergence as a public figure coincides with his decision to settle down in Calcutta, sometime in 1814. To an extent surely, the exodus from the countryside and mofussil towns to Calcutta was related to the pecuniary advantages that followed from an elementary knowledge of English. Rather than be thrust upon them, Bengali Hindus in particular, showed great eagerness and initiative in entering schools that taught English among other subjects. Some contemporary accounts have left behind vivid descriptions of how every morning, half-clad young boys would run beside the *palki* carrying the Scottish philanthropist David Hare (1775–1842) in the hope that they would be admitted to one of his several Free Schools. Another story still popular in Bengali households is that of the boy Vidyasagar who walked all the way from his native village Birsingha (in District Midnapore) to Calcutta, and obtained his first lessons in modern numerals by simply following the milestones fixed by the roadside. The moral of the story both then and now is that human character is fashioned by inquisitiveness and diligence.

In early colonial Calcutta, the knowledge of English was easily an aid to social esteem and professional success. On 21 April 1824, when Bishop Heber invited some prominent Bengalis of the city to his birthday party, he found them speaking English fluently and gracefully. Nitai Sen and Advaita Sen, two young schoolboys studying at Arratoon Petre's school in central Calcutta, were greatly respected in their locality even though they spoke only ungrammatical English. The knowledge of English did indeed lead to employment with the government or European mercantile houses. On the other hand, the great enthusiasm shown by upper-class Hindus for English medium education seems quite disproportionate to the number of jobs that such education might be reasonably expected to procure. In other words, a value was increasingly attached to what modern education could do to the intellectual constitution of man. In 1823, in a historic letter addressed to Governor-General Amherst, Rammohun Roy pleaded that official funds be utilized in the propagation of the 'useful knowledge' of the West in place of the speculative philosophical systems of the Hindus. Rammohun found the latter to be practically as useless as the medieval scholasticism of Europe.

By the 1830s and 1840s, schools set up almost exclusively through Indian efforts had become centres of an intellectual revolution. The best known instance of this is the Hindu College set up in 1817, which one contemporary described as 'the first national movement in the cause of improvement'. The finest minds among Hindu College students were deeply influenced by the life and thoughts of their favourite teacher, Henry Louis Vivian Derozio (1809–31). Derozio was appointed teacher at this institution when he was only seventeen years of age, and entrusted with the teaching of English, history, and classical literature. However, he was also known to organize weekly classes on the subjects of religion and metaphysics that were often attended by students in great numbers. As a teacher, Derozio always displayed a natural warmth and friendliness towards his students, often inviting them home and to unscheduled private meetings at extremely short notice. In his own assessment, however, his most important contribution was to make his students think for themselves. The *Calcutta Christian Observer* of August 1832 noted how the students of Hindu College 'had acquired a remarkable degree of courage and spirit in especially their opinion on all subjects ... Reason was now promoted to be a God and custom voted to be the idol of fools ...' Indeed, a strongly rational outlook upon life came to characterize College students in contemporary Calcutta. Thomas Paine's *Age of Reason* was an instant success and the story goes that an enterprising bookseller of the city managed to sell copies of this work at five times its stated price. Over time, this radical and dissenting streak in Derozio and some of his students became a matter of concern for parents who had sent their boys to Hindu College. In 1831, they forced the Managing Committee (which anyhow had more conservatives than reformers as members) to dismiss Derozio from his position as teacher. Under the influence of their teacher, the close followers of Derozio, also referred to as Derozians or Young Bengal, established several academic or quasi-academic bodies whose main purpose was to debate or discuss the major currents of thinking in contemporary Europe. To this category belong bodies like the Academic Association (1828) and the Society for the Acquisition of General Knowledge (1838). Also interesting are the new ideas, values, and mannerisms that came to be associated with the new class of students. A College boy, for instance, was taken to be always truthful. Dakshinaranjan Mukhopadhyay (1814–85), a member of Young Bengal, was once able to persuade a reluctant

Ramtanu Lahiri (1813–98), a friend and also a product of Hindu College, to accept a glass of sherry offered by Derozio's sister as refusing a lady would have been considered grossly impolite.

Another development also more distinctive to Calcutta than to adjacent towns or mofussil areas was the birth of the *madhyabitta*, literally meaning the middling classes. The madhyabitta had been noticed by a Bengali weekly, the *Bangadoot,* as early as 1829. Some forty years later, the *Amrit Bazar Patrika*, another important daily, used it interchangeably with the term 'middle class', calling it the most productive and dependable class that was potentially capable of revolutionizing Bengali society. However, the analogy offered here is somewhat misleading. Unlike their counterparts in Europe, the Bengali middle classes were hardly connected with the process of material production and did not enjoy a comparable measure of autonomy. Nevertheless, what led Indians to draw such false parallels was the misplaced belief that the historical experiences of Western societies could be replicated even in colonial India through universally potent laws. Such comparisons were particularly inept in the case of Bengal where a vastly unequal command over resources had all but wiped out the artisan and trading classes. Colonial Bengal also did not produce a class of merchant capitalists, who, at the opportune hour, could take to modern industrial entrepreneurship. In this respect, the experiences of western and southern India were significantly different from those of Bengal.

The madhyabitta of colonial Bengal did, however, produce an aristocracy of talent. A high percentage of this class was associated with the modern professions of law, print technology and book trade, journalism, literary production, and service under the government. They were behind the remarkable cultural awakening that characterized mid-nineteenth century Bengal, the movement for social and religious reform, and the first stirrings of nationalist sentiments. In Bankim's day, a term often used in relation to the madhyabitta was *bhadralok*, literally translated as the genteel folk. Generally speaking, the bhadralok were Western-educated, associated with the modern professions, and drawn from the three upper castes of Brahman, Baidya, and Kayastha. However, recent research has also revealed some of its inner structural tensions. For one, there was obviously a class dimension to this category. Thus, a Brahman Deputy Magistrate such as Bankim Chandra himself, drawing a reasonably good monthly salary could not be put in the same category as a fellow Brahman subsisting on a clerical salary. Interestingly enough, hierarchies built on caste could dilute this class aspect. A Deputy Magistrate by the name of Adhar Lal Sen from the ritually inferior Subarnabanik caste and a follower of Sri Ramakrishna Paramahamsa (1836–86), was once quite offended when upper-caste fellow devotees refused to dine at his house.

There is now scholarly consensus around the view that the term 'Renaissance' does not aptly describe the nature or extent of intellectual or cultural changes in early and mid-nineteenth century Bengal. Unlike Europe, the Bengal Renaissance witnessed neither a meaningful transformation of the society and economy, nor new political ideologies or forms of government. Rather, it was almost entirely founded on efforts to develop a new Bengali language and literature, and to reform religious ideas and practices of the Bengali Hindus. For a considerable length of time, there were no meaningful contributions to the fields of art, architecture, sculpture, or music that had indeed been the case in early modern Europe. Bankim Chandra himself believed that Indian patrons of art would do well to commission European rather than Indian artists. That apart, the Bengal Renaissance was very largely the work of one specific community—the Hindu bhadralok; the Bengali Muslims were drawn into it reluctantly and much later. Occupationally, a vast majority of Bengali Muslims were peasants and artisans, and concentrated in east Bengal, at a considerable distance from Calcutta. When compared to the Hindus, they were considerably poorer and less literate. While students of Hindu College paid their fees, those admitted to the Calcutta Madrasa (founded in 1781) had to be granted stipends by the government.

Here, it is also important to remember that for much of the nineteenth century, the traditional Muslim élite and the British ruling classes distrusted each other. 'We took India from the Mohamedans', an official noted in 1832, '... and the Mohammedans are most discontented. ... I do not say that

Muslims have extinguished all hopes of expelling us ... On the contrary, I believe that such hopes do exist in the breasts of many of the higher Mohammedans'. The same official was to conclude on the note that the Hindu 'were considerably more attached to our rule than the Mohammedan'. In hindsight, such apprehensions do not appear entirely misplaced. After Delhi was occupied by the British in 1804, a class of local Ulamas (Muslim theologians) issued a *fatwa* (a religious proclamation) against them and declared India to be unfit for true Muslims. This led to a series of military conflicts between the British and the Muslim aristocracy, especially around the north-west frontier of India. By the 1840s, under the influence of such leaders and theologians, even the Muslim peasantry of Bengal and Bihar was drawn into strongly anti-British movements and millenarian dreams about the restoration of a more just social order. Upper class Muslims everywhere resented the loss of political power and showed little intentions of accepting the new educational system. This visible inequality between the two major religious communities in India was soon to have important consequences. By the third quarter of the nineteenth century, the Hindus had advanced considerably more than the Muslims in the fields of modern education and professional employment. This led some Muslims to believe that they had been unjustly treated both by the government as well as the professionally advanced Hindus. Among educated Hindus, on the other hand, such disparities only reinforced the idea, introduced by colonialist history-writing, that Indo-Muslim rule represented a dark and regressive chapter in Indian history. From Rammohun down to Bankim, this idea surfaces with surprising regularity; the Hindu Bengali press of the time even claimed that it was the coming of the British that first threw an intellectual and moral challenge to the Hindu.

By the last decades of the nineteenth century, educated Hindus had begun to see the incongruity between their rich historical heritage and the abject state of social existence at the time. In part, this had grown out of their historical self-awareness as a people to which men like Sir William Jones, Thomas Colebrooke, Horace Hayman Wilson, and a host of other British scholars had made significant contributions. These scholars had researched extensively into Indian history, languages and literature, religion and philosophy, art, architecture, and archeology, and came to the conclusion that early India had witnessed significant developments in all these fields. Over time, this created a new pride of race and nostalgia among Hindus, and gave them greater self-confidence. Alongside, an increasing exposure to the social and political ideologies of contemporary Europe taught educated Hindus to develop a language of rights. Above all, the more sensitive minds were already beginning to sense the incompatibility between continuing colonial extraction and the prospects of Indian development. As India began to acquire a pivotal position within the British Empire, it also became subject to greater political and bureaucratic control. More money was spent on further strengthening the instruments of colonial control like the army and police than on developing Indian agriculture and industry. The 1870s and 1880s also saw a sharp rise in racial discrimination, and a palpable desire to reinforce the hiatus between the rulers and the ruled. Indians were disallowed to carry arms on their person and strictures were passed on the Indian language press. Tightening British control over key sectors like trade, finance, and industry left virtually no room for Indian enterprise. While the Census figures for 1881 reveal that a number of small private establishments were owned by the Kayastha, Tili, Teli, and Sadgop castes, only seven of the 105 companies registered in Calcutta had Indians as directors. An increasing number of graduates produced by the universities remained unemployed. By 1881, there were 1,700 graduates in Bengal and of these, as many as 635 were unemployed. Taken together, such changes explain why educated Indians and Bengalis began to grow more vocal.

The first flush of Bengali patriotism was not necessarily anti-British. Several leading thinkers and public figures in the province seemed to have uncritically accepted the 'providential' nature of British rule. Alhough this was more common among educated Hindus, similar voices could be occasionally heard even among the Muslims. Such sentiments are clearly indicated in the *Riyad-as-Salatin* (1788) of Gholam Hussain Salim (d. 1817), in the writings of Kazan-al-Qureshi (alias Kaikobad, 1858–1951), and Meer Mossarraf Hossain (1848–1911). Even in the 1870s and 1880s, Bankim Chandra himself and the conservative Hindu writer, Bhudeb Mukhopadhyay (1827–94) were arguing that it was not foreign rule per se that the Hindus opposed but bad governance. Bankim's *Anandamath* ends on the note that British rule would continue so long as Indians (read Hindus) had not perfected themselves in knowledge and power. Importantly, such views were also increasingly under attack from people who were deeply familiar with the West and Western life. A classic case here is that of Aurobindo Ghosh (1887–1950), who spent a good part of his childhood and youth in England. For Aurobindo, bodies like the Indian National Congress were making too much noise about too little; it was also fairly evident that polite petitioning was not going to yield very much. He wanted such methods to be substituted by deeper introspection and a militant call to patriotic duty. An idea quite apparent in the writings of both Sri Aurobindo and Bankim was that of conquest of the self, the courage to admit that the actual enemy was not some force external to oneself but one's own selfishness, sentimentalism, and cowardice. This represented a turn from a feeble request for certain civic concessions to a manly assertion of one's rights and duties. The emphasis was now increasingly upon self-help and self-sufficiency; Indians were called upon to start their own economic enterprises and themselves produce the goods they wished to consume rather than depend on those imported from England. The former, it was argued, would help them retain profits made from trade and industry within India while the latter would only drain Indian wealth. In Bengal itself, the gospel of *swadeshi* (promoting the indigenous) was in circulation by the 1860s though its more militant use was to come some forty years later. In the late nineteenth century, the swadeshi idea was also extended to the fields of education and culture. There was now a new enthusiasm for rediscovering forgotten ways of life and culture, a new pride in the use of the vernacular as against the English language, and a new moral commitment towards the community and the nation. With ideas of self-help and self-sufficiency increasingly becoming the new mantra, political battlelines naturally came to be drawn afresh.

## The Cultural World of Nineteenth Century Bengal and Bankim Chandra

The intellectual life of Bankim Chandra Chattopadhyay was critically determined by the cultural world he inherited. Linguistic innovation, developing new literary genres like the Bengali novel, a pressing anxiety to redefine the religious and cultural identity of Hindus or the counter-offensive against crude European readings of India had all surfaced in Bengali public life before him. On the other hand, it could be reasonably claimed that to each of these, Bankim Chandra imparted a new outlook. Bankim, for instance, was by no means the first Bengali novelist and yet few novelists before or after his time have enjoyed comparable levels of popularity. Again, if realism is taken to be one of the defining features of the novel, Bankim would not be the best example to follow. Indeed, one of the points of criticism persistently levelled against him was that his novels did not draw upon characters that one could realistically hope to locate in contemporary Bengali society. Surely, if his works had dealt only in bizarre tales of adventure and saucy romances, the alleged non-realism of Bankim's characters might have been more easily overlooked. In truth, all but one of Bankim's fifteen novels were set in Bengal, and of these, some were intended to be intense family dramas with underlying moral lessons. The irony of it though is that contemporary novelists like Taraknath Gangopadhyay (1843–91), who did bring greater realism into his plots or characterization, were nowhere as popular as Bankim Chandra. And, while the average Bengali of the time may have failed to find himself in Bankim's novels, he still read these with avid interest. It might be justly suggested, therefore, that perhaps Bankim Chandra's popularity as a novelist rested on a palpable swing in public moods, away from commonplace realism and towards one that was idyllic and privately coveted.

An important element, that Bankim was perhaps the first to introduce into his novels, was pre-marital romance. Scholars of Bengali literature are generally agreed on the view that this was quite unknown in pre-modern Bengali works of fiction. A romantic relationship between man and woman was expected to commence only following marriage and to flower through the long years of conjugal life. Up to a point, Bankim seems to have agreed with this, especially given the widespread practices of early betrothals and marriage. He himself was married the first time to a girl of five and remained strongly nostalgic about his child bride. At the same time, he apparently had the sensitivity and courage to reveal the mutual attraction between men and women even outside marital life that orthodox society may have privately found titillating but did everything to suppress in public life. This new sensitivity in Bankim Chandra was derived from his reading of European literature. What proved to be more distinctive to him was the conservatism he brought into play even when acknowledging the appeal or power of socially transgressive romantic love. In at least two of his novels, *Bishbriksha* (1873) and *Krishna Kanter Will* (1878), Bankim Chandra reveals the secret passions of Hindu widows and of men drawn into clandestine relationships with women outside their married lives. Since such clandestine thoughts or feelings invariably ended in death or disaster, one would have to say that here, Bankim was not really playing the role of the reformer trying to persuade his society to be more kindly or forgiving towards the secret desires of the heart or even momentary acts of indiscretion. On the contrary, it is his conservatism that deliberately forecloses other possible conclusions to such passionate human drama. In a sense, Bankim exposed the underbelly of a society without simultaneously developing a genuine empathy for the victims he portrayed. He did not have the compassion of the reformer Iswar Chandra Vidyasagar, who wept uncontrollably at the sight of the child widow or the spiritual grace of Sri Ramakrishna Paramahamsa, which could treat the sinner or the socially despised with love and kindness.

Bankim was clearly didactic in his novels, though over time, this took two somewhat different forms. One of these was socially puritanical and found unbridled passion to be always fraught with tragic consequences. The other, arriving slightly later in time, attempted a subtle combination of a traditional spiritual discipline with modern patriotism. In his novels, *Anandamath*, *Devi Chaudhurani* (1884), and *Sitaram* (1887), Bankim emerges as philosopher–patriot trying to rest patriotism on the older Hindu concept of selfless action (*nishkam karma*).

So far, we have often referred to Bankim's popularity as a novelist without also trying to assess just who his numerous readers might have been. All novels produced by Bankim underwent reprints though not with the same frequency or comparable commercial success. His relatively short works like *Jugalanguriya* (1874), *Indira* (1873), or *Radharani* (1876) do not usually figure in any serious analysis of his fiction. On the other hand, the novels that attained by far the greatest popularity were not necessarily also his best works of fiction. A good example here would be that of *Anandamath* itself, which was immensely popular but in the opinion of many a critic, overly contrived. It would be reasonable to suggest that his readership tended to change over the years, partly in keeping with changes in public mood but also as a result of what Bankim chose to portray in his novels. At least initially, his readership may have been drawn mostly from women and adolescents who found old-style, Sanskritic Bengali both unintelligible and far from entertaining. As this class was not quite familiar with English and had no cultural problems taking to vernacular works, they found in Bankim's works a whole new world of aesthetic joy and entertainment. This would be particularly true of the first two novels, *Durgeshnandini* (1865) and *Kapala Kundala* (1866). These were romances that kept the reader's attention riveted on fairly dramatic narratives. Bankim's readership changed somewhat when beginning with the *Bishbriksha*, his novels began to be serialized in the journal *Bangadarshan* that he founded in 1872. *Bangadarshan* was a journal with a serious scholarly output. It carried articles on popular science, history and culture, reviews of books, book notices, and other features of literary interest. The serialization of novels in the *Bangadarshan* may have split Bankim's readership, as allowing for exceptions, women and adolescents would have been less drawn to learned essays than to the novels. On the other hand, surely, the novel now penetrated the entire household with people perhaps reading it by turns. Also, among the more regular readers, serialized appearances may have further intensified the anxiety to gather which way the story would turn in the subsequent numbers. Apparently, the *Bangadarshan* rendered great service to both the world of Bengali journalism and to the Bengali novel.

* * *

It would be somewhat misleading to suggest that Bankim's standing as a modern writer and thinker rested entirely on his works of fiction. Brilliant and vastly entertaining as these might well have been, they still comprise only a part of his great intellectual output. If it had been Bankim's intention to remain exclusively a novelist, he might have ended up by contributing a few more. In truth, he was also a major essayist and spent a good part of his private time in editing and publishing two fairly successful journals, the *Bangadarshan* and the *Prochar*. On a rough count, he contributed over a hundred essays in the Bengali and the English languages, not counting those that later made up his two major treatises, *Dharmatattwa* and *Krishna Charitra*. It is in these essays that we really locate Bankim Chandra the thinker and come to terms with the essential substance and trajectories of his social and political thought. In fact, there is good reason to believe that after a point in time, Bankim Chandra considered novel writing to be a part of a larger cultural project. The novels *Anandamath*, *Devi Chaudhurani*, and *Sitaram* are, in a sense, dramatic enactments of ideas that he had consistently expressed in several essays. For Bankim, however, writing was also a means of self-discovery and self-expression. He wrote not just for the sheer joy of writing though that was by no means unimportant, but to discover some hidden meaning in his very life and existence. As the Guru in *Dharmatattwa* remarks, '*Ei jeebon loiya kee koribo*?' ('What am I to do with this life?'). For Bankim, this appears to have been a question that transcended commonplace needs or desires.

As with some prominent thinkers before him, Bankim's cultural project tried to keep clear of the two extremes of an uncritical acceptance of Westernization and a xenophobic rejection of all that was not Indian. However, he would have also known that this was not a position which could be easily determined and retained over a long time. Before him, Raja Rammohun Roy had displeased both the orthodox Hindus and his Christian friends by suggesting that

'Unitarianism' (theologically, the idea of an indivisible Godhead) could be the defining feature for both Hinduism and Christianity. Tactically, Rammohun was forced to consistently bring into his life and thought two related considerations. First, even when upholding some kind of religious universalism, he tried to rest it as far as possible on Hindu cultural moorings. Thus, one of his last works, *The Universal Religion*, used the culturally innocuous term 'Supreme Being' to describe God; on the other hand, the texts upon which Rammohun based his arguments in the same work were almost exclusively Hindu–Brahmanical in origin. Secondly, he was more prepared to bring greater radicalism in purely religious matters than in the social. At religious congregations of the Brahmo Sabha (which Rammohun had founded in 1828), Vedic texts would be recited from a secluded spot by orthodox Brahmans. Rammohun ridiculed the polytheism of Puranic religion (Vaishnavism in particular) but would not forsake his caste identity as a Brahman. Understandably, the cautious and selective reformism of Rammohun irked the more uncompromising Derozians. One of them described the Rammohun faction thus:

> Before the bigots, they are bigots, before the liberals, they are liberals, before the Whigs, they are Whigs and before the Tories, they are Tories.

Rammohun himself would have been appalled at the way some students of Hindu College took matters to the extreme. 'If there be anything under heaven that I or my friends look upon with most abhorrence,' declared the Derozian, Madhav Chandra Mallik, 'it is Hinduism'. Rammohun's mission, if anything, was the very opposite. Essentially, it argued that when shorn of its irrationalities or excesses, Hinduism could not only be given a new lease of life but also proclaimed as one of the finest religions in the world. The thesis (which gathered greater strength and momentum by the late nineteenth century) that Hinduism had been deliberately corrupted over time by certain vested interests, probably originated with Rammohun. Rammohun is believed to be the first modern Indian to have used the term 'Hinduism' to collectively describe a wide range of religious beliefs and practices associated with the Hindus. Evidently, Rammohun was trying to forge together a pan-Indian community of Hindus, united in thought and deed as against local communities often separated by religious sectarianism. Perhaps this might partly explain why Rammohun rested his religious reformation on highly philosophical texts like the Upanishads rather than the Puraṇas which formed the textual basis of several religious cults or communities.

Predictably, it was Rammohun's attempt at social reformation (as for instance, the prohibition of sati) that first rallied orthodox Hindus against him. The latter had no major problem in accepting Rammohun's zeal for theological reform for, after all, monotheism (the idea of one God) had been no less known to the Hindu–Brahmanical tradition. In truth, orthodox Hindu society in his day would have drawn some comfort from the way the reformed Church of Rammohun was effectively keeping young men from converting to Christianity. Looking back at those years it might be justly claimed that the parting of ways between the Hindu and Brahmo came when under Keshab Chunder Sen (1838–84), the Brahmo Samaj attempted to create a legally distinct community of Brahmos, with their own rites and usages. The legal prohibition of sati in 1829 was nevertheless a big shock to orthodox sensibilities, especially as the reformist party claimed that the practice had no sanction in Hindu religion. The oppositionists rallied together under what they called the 'Dharma Sabha' (founded in 1830), which even tried, albeit unsuccessfully, to get the British Parliament to quash the law against sati. The Dharma Sabha has sometimes been called the first proto-nationalist body in India for the way in which it resisted an 'unwarranted' intervention of the colonial government in the beliefs and practices of its non-Christian subjects. In truth, it was more in the nature of a faction or pressure group which wanted to protect some vested interests. Among the oppositionists of the 1829 law were disgruntled zamindars who were unhappy at the government's resumption of rent-free (*lakhiraj*) lands. A few years later, the Sabha also tried to bribe prominent citizens of Calcutta so that they would not attend a public function hosted by a gentleman from the reformist party.

However, from this it would be unfair to conclude that the conservatives were, in principle, opposed to all progressive changes in social and educational matters or for that matter, in collaborating with the English. Sir Radhakanta Deb (1784–1867), Rammohun's principal opponent and leader of the Dharma Sabha, was also Director of Hindu College for over thirty years, an important functionary of the Calcutta School Society and the Calcutta School Book Society, both of which had several European members, and the co-author of a manual on female education called *Stri Shiksha Vidhayak* (1822). The radicals, on the other hand, were often known to go back on their radicalism. Derozio accused one of his students, Prasanna Kumar Tagore, of keeping double standards. Prasanna Kumar, who ran the reformist journal, *The Reformer*, denouncing idolatry, was found to join Durga Puja festivities at home. On this, a friend, later writing on his behalf, was to candidly confess that 'The property that he (Prasanna Kumar) inherits from his ancestors is left to him on conditions of celebrating the Pooja every year. Under the circumstances, what is he to do!'

The turn towards radicalism met with opposition from various quarters. Men like Radhakanta Deb consistently tried to drive a wedge between accepting English education and English ideas. The first in his view was functionally useful, the second, socially unsettling. Interestingly, some support for the orthodox position also came from the local English press; in 1831, the *India Gazette*, criticized young Bengalis for 'unnecessarily running counter to the customs and institutions of the native society'. In the opinion of yet others, instances of Hindus severing their roots from society only further encouraged the 'slandering' of Hinduism by non-Hindus. Here, obviously, accusations were being levelled against the Christian missionaries who were allowed to enter India in greater numbers after 1813. The cultural threat from Christian missionary propaganda was already evident by Rammohun's time, for, during the period between 1821–3, Rammohun published four numbers of the *Brahmanical Magazine or the Missionary and the Brahman,* contesting Evangelist accusations against India and Indians. In 1823, in a rare show of unity, the conservatives and reformers came together to start the Gaudiya Samaj (Bengali

Society), one of whose chief objectives was to prevent missionary propaganda from attracting young minds.

The tactical error that the orthodox party committed was in naively believing that the spread of modern education could be confined to purely vocational uses. In reality, the very opposite happened. The spread of such education in the new schools and colleges opened up a whole new world for young men and, to a lesser extent, for women. It aroused a sense of intellectual interest or curiosity, and enabled students to read deeply into the political, social, and philosophical currents of thought that were agitating the modern world. After 1820, this became even more possible as the Calcutta School Book Society obtained permission to provide Bengali translations of English literary and scientific works published by the London Society for the Diffusion of Useful Knowledge. All the same, there still existed a correlationship between a command over the English language and familiarity with contemporary developments. For one, Continental thinkers could be read only in English, and among the works by popular English thinkers themeselves, not all would be available in translation. Presumably, the more affluent among the English educated maintained good personal libraries. As was once the case with the merchant aristocracy of Florence, Venice, or Genoa, works of art and personal libraries became important indices of social rank and a cultural requirement for the upwardly mobile. In one of Bankim's novels, *Radharani,* even a woman is shown to possess such a personal library.

By the second half of the nineteenth century though, the two most popular streams of thought were those of Utilitarianism and Positivism. The first, however, had been known to Indians for a relatively longer time. One of Rammohun's early biographers, Kissory Chand Mitra, called Rammohun a 'religious Benthamite' because of the somewhat instrumentalist view that he took of religion and religious life. In Rammohun's understanding, rather than enjoying an autonomous value or function, religion was validated largely by its abilty to render socially useful functions. From the relevant records, it is known that when in England, Rammohun called upon the English Utiliatarian philosopher, Jeremy Bentham, who, in turn, is said to have found in his visitor, an 'intensely admired and dearly loved collaborator in the service of mankind'. The only major issue that seems to have separated Rammohun from Utiliatarian thinking is his deep respect for tradition. Utilitarian philosophy, guided as it was by considerations of practical utility, was notoriously opposed to tradition that was taken to be of little contemporary value. Rammohun, on the contrary, believed that traditions modernize or at least that they could be made to suitably modernize.

With respect to Utilitarianism, this was broadly the position that Bankim Chandra also took. Usefulness was indeed the yardstick by which to measure the value or credibility of social or cultural institutions. At the same time, he did not believe that judgements on this account could be arrived at hastily. As in the case of Rammohun, Bankim's self-awareness as an upper-caste Hindu came in the way of his overly criticizing Indian tradition. By this time, however, Utilitarianism had also come to be associated with many more socio-political institutions. The writings of John Stuart Mill (1806–73), for example, had transformed it from crude hedonism to high levels of philosophical sophistication. Historically, it also came to be associated with liberal ideology that championed individualism, gender equality, and a free press. One of Bankim's early essays, *Samya* ('Egalitarianism', 1872) very faithfully reflects such currents of belief. Chapter 5 of this work, for instance, is virtually a summary of Mill's *Subjection of Women* (1868). In later life, however, Bankim confessed to have gone back on these views, even though as he somewhat cynically noted, 'such ideas sold very well'. The *Samya*, incidentally, was never reprinted in its original form and in one of his other works, *Kamalakanto* (1885), Bankim had reason to equate Utility with crass materialism (*'udar darshan'*). All the same, his differences with Mill or Utilitarianism should not be over-stretched. Although increasingly sceptical of Mill's views, Bankim wrote a touching obituary on the philosopher's death in 1873 wherein he was described as a 'close relative'(*nikat atmiya*).

The problems that Bankim may have had with Utilitarianism and the values that it advocated are, in all probability, related to his growing conservatism in social matters. In *Dharmatattwa*, the idea of an equality between sexes meets with some ridicule. But perhaps, more importantly, Bankim's discomfiture is also related to the strong individualism in Mill, which, in the Indian context, he found both irresponsible and mischievous. It might surprise some to hear that Bankim did not quite support the Indian agitation against press censorship imposed by the colonial government, and in a more general sense, he was also worried that individualism, when taken too far, would visibly affect the more pressing task of social integration. Utilitarianism, as he might have found, tended to under-value the power of selflessness and idealism.

In hindsight, it would appear as though Bankim found an effective antidote to the excesses of individualism in the Positivist philosophy of August Comte (1798–1857). Positivism in Bengal had been intitally confined to some English civil servants and in some respects, it was markedly different from the ideas or values it was associated with on the European continent. For instance, the presence of Europeans in Indian Positivist clubs blunted an anti-colonial sentiment that was very much a part of Positivist thinking elsewhere. On the other hand, it must also be said that the Indian admirers of Positivism too used Comte and his views quite selectively, and gave it a different character. One of the prominent Indians to pioneer this change was Jogendra Chandra Ghosh (1842–1902), an affluent zamindar by occupation. In general, Indian Positivism paid greater attention to sociological ideas within Positivism than the scientific ones. They treated it more as a philosophical system than a method of empirical investigation. Jogendra Chandra himself tried to wed Positivism to a somewhat backward-looking, Brahmanical revival. In a subsequent chapter, we shall also see how Bankim Chandra faulted Positivism on account of its omitting matters like God and religion.

Positivist philosophy especially appealed to those who were on the side of restraint and caution. Comte and the Positivists advocated evolutionary change as against revolutionary change. Comte's major work, *Cours De Philosphie Positive* (6 vols., 1830–42) presented a blueprint for human development which was to progress through three stages—the Metaphysical, the Religious, and the Positive. The last represented the sublimation of the human powers of the mind and body, and man's fullest integration with society. In Positivism, therefore, there was both a turning back on revolutionary change and the tendency to uphold the community over the individual. Positivism may have also proved attractive for men like Jogendra Chandra and Bankim because of the way in which it allowed them to defend the indigenous tradition without being overly apologetic about it. Change was indeed admitted within this philosophy, but one that was largely self-determined and in keeping with the cultural preferences of the people.

In the cultural history of nineteenth century Bengal, Bankim Chandra Chattopadhyay may be seen to stand at the threshold of two inter-related and extremely significant questions. What, after all, was the modern Indian to accept from the West and in what manner? The obverse of this question was to try and determine what part of the tradition that he inherited could be most vitally defended against the critical moral and cultural challenges from the West. To both these questions Bankim Chandra tried to offer answers that appeared to him to be the most practical and plausible under the circumstances. These were peculiarly his answers and may be said to have differed from other solutions offered within contemporary Indian thinking. The other set of questions with which he was forced to engage himself concerned the political fate of India and Indians. One of the issues on which he deliberated the most was the inter-relationship between freedom in a purely political sense and that in the moral and social sense. One feels that the worldview of Bankim Chandra can be approached more closely through an expression he once used himself—'non-political patriotism'. Bankim rued the fact that India had lost her political autonomy and freedom; on the other hand, he did not believe that this could be truly restored until every Indian was morally and intellectually free.

# 2

## A Life Lived in Fullness

He (Bankim) could not be called a guru since he preached no spiritual precepts; no one dared to call him a friend either. And yet, everybody seemed to love and respect him and would feel immensely gratified to hear from him. Unless Bankim Babu himself had put in a word of praise, no writing would be considered good.

—Haraprasad Sastri (Translated)

Bankim Chandra Chattopadhyay was the third of four sons born to Jadav Chandra Chattopadhyay, a Brahman of the Rarhi sub-caste settled in Kanthalpara (district Hoogly, West Bengal). In his professional life, Jadav Chandra rose to the position of Deputy Collector, retiring from government service in 1875. The Chattopadhyays of Kanthalpara were a fairly well-known family in the neighbourhood and insofar as the Brahman community of Lower Bengal was concerned, any discreet enquiries about a 'Raibahadur' residing in the area would invariably point to Jadav Chandra who had been conferred with this honorary title by the Bengal government.

Jadav Chandra's own life had been quixotic and marked by dramatic incidents. Once, when reprimanded by his father for an act of ritual impropriety, he left home to join an older brother at Jajpur (Orissa). When barely eighteen, he contracted a mysterious and severe illness, and at one point of time was given up for dead. Miraculously, however, he was revived at the cremation grounds by a holy man who is said to have accurately predicted his service under the government but particularly, the birth of a son who would bring great glory to the family. Ascetics, holy men, and miracles abound in the novels of Bankim Chandra. Thus there is Abhiram Swami in *Durgeshnandini* (1865), Madhavacharya in *Mrinalini* (1869), the Kapalik in *Kapala Kundala* (1866), the Brahmachari in *Bishbriksha* (1873), Ramanand Swami in *Chandrashekhar* (1875), the Physician in *Anandamath* (1882), Bhavani Pathak in *Devi Chaudhurani* (1884) and Gangadhar Swami in *Sitaram* (1887). In the novel, *Rajani* (1877), a sanyasi restores eyesight to a blind girl and in *Anandamath* again, Kalyani's daughter, given up for dead after being bitten by a snake, is miraculously brought back to life.

All of Jadav Chandra's four sons served the government, though not in the same capacities or with comparable professional success. One of Bankim's elder brothers, Sanjib Chandra, fared rather poorly in his official career (it was rumoured that he once sneered at his English superior's poor knowledge of Bengali). Virtually nothing is known about the professional lives of the eldest, Shyama Charan, or the youngest, Purna Chandra. All the brothers, barring Shyama Charan, reveal some literary talent. Sanjib Chandra was a fairly successful travel writer and novelist; his *Bengal Ryots: Their Rights and Liabilities* (1864) deeply influenced Bankim's own writings on the peasantry (*Bongodesher Krishak* ['The Peasantry of Bengal']). Purna Chandra, Bankim's junior by about ten years, is considered by some to be the first short story writer in Bengali.

In 1865, Jadav Chandra initiated a long family feud by disinheriting two of his sons, Shyama Charan and Bankim Chandra, from their share in the family property. If this seems arbitrary and unjust, one would have to lay such charges against Bankim as well who similarly denied one of his daughters, Neelaj Kumari, from her share of his personal assets. There is no conclusive evidence to prove that Jadav Chandra's decision was guided by some unhappiness or ill-feeling towards the sons he so deprived. On the contrary, he apparently took pride in Bankim Chandra, India's first graduate, a civilian officer by profession, who was already exhibiting some extraordinary literary talent. Perhaps this decision had something to do with the respective professional and financial standing of his sons. More importantly though, Jadav Chandra's decision by itself did not permanently split the family or force the brothers to take sides. Bankim Chandra was always closer to Sanjib Chandra, who was a beneficiary under the will, than to Shyama Charan who was not. In fact, Shyama Charan and Bankim were never consistently on cordial terms. Even as late as 1887, when they were on a pilgrimage in north India, differences developed between the two, forcing Shyama Charan to cut short his trip. Bankim, however, had the goodness and grace to dedicate one novel each to his three brothers; *Durgeshnandini* to Shyama Charan, *Kapala Kundala* to Sanjib Chandra, and *Chandrashekhar* to Purna Chandra. In the 1880s, when he was completing the novel *Devi Chaudhurani,* he was also to claim that the concept of nishkam karma (selfless action) that he had applied to this novel, had actually been learnt from his father, Jadav Chandra. What Bankim Chandra truly resented was the burden of financial debts that his father had passed on to his sons. Ironically, even though he was denied his share in the family property, Bankim had to help repay with Shyama Charan a sum of over Rs 8,000. It was widely known in the locality that Jadav Chandra's earnings failed to match his extravagant habits. As the head of a respected family and as a civil servant, Jadav Chandra felt compelled to spend lavishly on community festivals, friends, and feasts. It has been suggested that such over-spending was intended to cover up the family's loss of ritual status in the past. We find this reflected even in Bankim's novels. In *Bishbriksha* and *Indira*, for example, there are fairly explicit references to how a little extra spending at the right places resolved most problems.

* * *

One of Bankim Chandra's early biographers, Shochondro Majumdar, tells us that Bankim considered himself to be a largely self-taught man. By his own reckoning, his childhood had been spent in the company of bad friends and lacked positive moral influences. His father, Bankim complained, would be mostly away on official duty, and his mother was much too old-fashioned to meet his intellectual demands. For a student who performed brilliantly in every examination he took, Bankim confessed to have been grossly inattentive and uninterested in his course of study. At Kanthalpara, he was entrusted to the care of a private tutor and when six, asked to join his father at Midnapore. On the recommendation of the headmaster, F. Tead, Jadav Chandra admitted him to the local English school. Here he spent the next four years, returning to Kanthalpara by the end of 1848. The following year, he was admitted to Mohsin College at Hoogly where he spent a little over seven years. In 1856, he was transferred to the Law Section at Presidency College, Calcutta. His academic performance through these years was outstanding. In 1854, he topped the list of students awarded a junior scholarship and two years later, he also topped the list of senior Scholarship holders. In 1857, he took the entrance examination to the Calcutta University, securing a first division and in 1858, he was awarded the B.A. degree of that University. That year, only two of the ten examinees came close to passing the degree examination. Bankim Chandra and one Jadu Nath Basu cleared five of the six papers but fell short of the sixth by seven marks. The University Syndicate eventually awarded both of them seven grace marks and placed them in the second division. Bankim and Jadu Nath thereby earned the distinction of being India's first graduates of a modern university.

Although keen to pursue a career in law, Bankim had to soon abandon the idea. Upon passing the examinations, he was promptly offered the post of Deputy Magistrate and Deputy Collector (Class V) by the then Lt. Governor of Bengal, Sir James Halliday. Jadav Chandra prevailed upon him to promptly accept the offer.

Bankim Chandra joined service under the government in August 1858, and for the next thirty-three years performed his official duties with distinction. Other than occupying the position of Deputy Magistrate and Deputy Collector for several districts, he was also appointed to the post of Personal Assistant to the Commissioners of Rajshahi and Burdwan divisions, as Secretary to a Commission for pay revision, and as Assistant Secretary to the Government of Bengal. The last position produced some public controversy as within a few months of Bankim's joining, the post was abruptly abolished, only to be later offered to a European. At the time, it was widely rumoured that this was the Bengal Secretariat's way of reprimanding Bankim for the 'seditious' intentions buried in his novels. Happily, those outside the bureaucracy did not share this view; even the English-owned paper, *The Statesman,* expressed surprise and unhappiness at the decision.

If one looks back at those years, it would appear as though Bankim's ascent up the official hierarchy was slow and halting. It took him five years to rise from Deputy Magistrate and Deputy Collector, Class V to Class IV, another seven years to Class II, and thereafter, an extraordinarily long fourteen years to ascend to Class I. This is indeed surprising, given the fact that he was considered one of the best 'native Deputies' in service. R.B. Chapman, the Commissioner of Howrah, found him 'singularly intelligent and capable though apt to theorize too much'. C.E. Buckland, who produced a valuable account of the administrative history of Bengal, recorded his important contribution to the suppression of river dacoities and the establishment of peace and order in the eastern canals. As a Magistrate, he was strict and upright, and contemporary accounts suggest that the police and prosecution were mostly reluctant to take cases to his court. Notwithstanding the fact that he was friendly with many Englishmen, the Lt. Governor Charles Elliot and Lady Elliot included, Bankim's modest professional success may have followed from the differences he often developed with his immediate superiors. The latter are known to have taken exception to Bankim's somewhat curt notings on files and his dignified refusal to unduly please higher placed officers. Thus, we hear of his differences with Mr Macaulay at the Secretariat, and with Magistrates Westamacott and Buckland, and his not offering salaam to Presidency Commissioner Monroe whom he once met at the Eden Gardens. A commonly enforced deterrent action against such 'erring' conduct then (as now) was transfer. Throughout his career, Bankim was kept on temporary assignments and sent on transfers at extremely short notice, some of which he may have truly resented. Not surprisingly, over the years, he developed a strong dislike for the world of the 'Deputy' (Magistrate), a vivid picture of which he presents to us in his *Muchiram Gud* (1884). This work clearly reveals the bitter lessons that he had learnt during his long years of government service. The likes of Deputy Muchiram, who deliberately wrote faulty English, never forgot to please his superiors, and readily admitted his subaltern status, made his way up the ladder with ease while self-respecting Indian officers suffered in obscurity. The plight of the efficient but self-respecting government servant that Bankim unravels in a work such as this reflects not just his personal saga but that of his class. In his short biographical sketches of the playwright Deenabandhu Mitra and his brother Sanjib Chandra, he reveals how these men got far less out of their official careers than they deserved. It is common knowledge that shortly after he started serializing *Anandamath* in his periodical *Bangadarshan*, Bankim Chandra was summoned by the Lt. Governor to answer charges of disloyalty. What is not as well known is that the government decided to drop charges on the basis of the testimony not of the author but that of Keshab Chandra Sen, once Bankim's classmate at Presidency College, and a man known for his strong sense of loyalty to the government. Following this, changes had to be made to the plot and character of the novel in its later editions. The rebel Santans could now be seen to fight Muslim armies, not British. A career in the government, Bankim often complained, had been the bane of his life and perhaps thoughts of how much better-off he would have been as an independent judge or lawyer often crossed his mind. Indeed the two men from Bengal that he most envied were Justices Romesh Chandra Mitter and Dwarka Nath Mitter.

However, it would be quite absurd to suggest, as indeed has been done on occasions, that Bankim took to novel writing out of a sense of frustration towards his official career. Bankim Chandra, as we know, published his first novel in 1865 and in March of the following year, was promoted to the rank of Deputy Magistrate and Deputy Collector, Class III. This was not a despairing man or a man already aggrieved at the tardy progress he was making in his profession. That feeling was to come later when he was already considered to be one of Bengal's finest novelists.

Bankim Chandra was married for the first time in 1849 to the five-year old Mohini. He lost her after ten years of married life, but within a few months of this tragic incident, was married again to Rajlakshmi Debi of Halishahr. Our sources reveal that Bankim had a long and happy married life with Rajlakshmi, and was a proud father of three daughters—Sharat Kumari, Neelaj Kumari and Utpal Kumari. Interestingly though, there are, at places, subtle suggestions of some feminine influence upon Bankim outside his second marriage. One possibility here is that Bankim Chandra deeply loved his child bride, Mohini, and continued to privately mourn her loss. Perhaps it is of her that he writes:

> It appears as though childhood romances are always ill-fated. How many of those whom you had loved as a child re-appear in your youthful dreams? Or even live long enough for that!
>
> (Translated from *Chandrashekhar*)

That true love was by nature elusive and painful is a suggestion that repeatedly appears in Bankim Chandra's novels. The other possibility is an act of youthful indiscretion that Bankim may have committed and about which he remained somewhat guilt-ridden. The novel *Bishbriksha*, by his own admission, carried an autobiographical element, and those familiar with the story will realize that here he could have been referring to Nagendra who is drawn into an extra-marital relationship but was eventually re-united with his wife, Suryamukhi. Such conjectures about Bankim's personal life enable us to better understand the sharply conflicting positions that he often took with respect to women. With him, a woman was both an object of love and sexual attraction, and a self-effacing housewife. Her innate strength and beauty could break homes, but could also be the source of enduring conjugal happiness. Here, his first wife or the unidentifiable woman about whom Bankim has only tangentially hinted, personified beauty and romantic love, unburdened by routine domestic responsibilities. The second wife, with whom Bankim spent thirty years, represented all that he expected of an ideal Hindu wife—fidelity, faith, and forbearance. It was her unwavering inner strength that served as the perfect foil to his nervous energy. In the novel *Krishna Kanter Will*, what the character Gobindalal, also tormented by his attraction for two women, observes may well be true of Bankim himself:

> The woman is the exemplar of kindness and forgiveness. She represents God's most sublime creation, His very shadow on earth. The woman represents light of which the man is a mere shadow. Can light ever forsake shadow?
>
> (Translated from *Krishna Kanter Will*)

* * *

The standard sources on the life and work of Bankim Chandra appear to be in agreement over certain points. For instance, nearly all testimonies left behind by close friends and contemporaries speak of his attractive appearance—slim, tall, and upright with a penetrating gaze. Also quite evident are his habits of order and cleanliness. Not a speck of dust could be found on his desk, and Bankim invariably remembered to clean up his quills before retiring for the day. He was also a habitual smoker of the hookah and in happier days, when differences within the family had not yet erupted over Jadav Chandra's will, weekend visitors to the family house at Kanthalpara would often find all four brothers smoking away amidst absorbing gossip and merriment. In his early life, Bankim insisted on using a knife and fork at the dinner table but soon realized that when it came to handling Bengali culinary delights, these were of little practical value. Sometimes, however, he took his convictions to frivolous extremes. Offended at the allegations levelled against the 'frail' Bengali, Bankim, for a time, took to the extraordinary daily diet of four chickens and twice that number of eggs. In his personal tastes, he remained fairly anglicized. Bankim's living room revealed the use of expensive European decorative pieces and the choicest contemporary furniture. Imposing oil paintings of himself and those of his father hung from the walls and a harmonium, a recent import to Calcutta, was prominently displayed in a corner. Bankim was known to occasionally play on this instrument and later used it to teach elementary musical notes to his grandson. He certainly appears to have been musically inclined and especially drawn to the melodious Vaishnava *kirtans*. Verses from the medieval Vaishnava poets of Bengal that he often heard from wandering kirtan-singers were later suitably inserted into his fiction. The two better-known examples of this are the verses from the *Gita Gobinda* that are repeatedly sung by the rebels in *Anandamath*, and the particularly moving couplet from an unnamed poet in which a love-afflicted woman, in order to avoid exposure, passes off her tears of anguish as tears produced by a smoky kitchen stove.

By nature, Bankim Chandra was restless and nervous, and quite reluctant to be drawn to any form of physical exercise. He feared danger from stray cattle, preferred playing cards to a brisk walk, and even after joining government service, could not bring himself to ride a horse. At Midnapore, as a boy of barely seven, Bankim preferred to fall into conversation with his European hostess rather than play with children of his age. On the other hand, a rare boldness and unflinching self-respect never deserted him. Once, at the residence of the local Deputy Magistrate Molett, Bankim felt greatly offended when someone came out to call the English boys to tea but not him. He never visited the Moletts again. His youngest brother, Purna Chandra best brings out this paradoxical side to Bankim Chandra's character. Despite his unadventurous nature, Bankim was known to have carried out some extraordinary feats. A furious storm when he was on a boat in mid-stream never scared him. In his official career, he is known to have overpowered an Englishman with a fully loaded pistol despite being unarmed himself. Although not keen to enforce this upon himself, Bankim Chandra certainly acknowledged the importance of physical culture. His *Dharmatattwa* (1888) took this to be integral to man's all-round development.

Had it not been for his inner resolve and courage, Bankim would have found it difficult to cope with the several challenges that arose in the course of his long career. Besides hard-to-please superiors and inefficient subordinates, he also had to put up with several rogues and scoundrels, who sought immunity from the law on account of their race and status. In 1861, that is, barely three years after joining government service, he had to face the wrath of Morrel, a particularly notorious indigo planter of Khulna and his henchman, Denis Hely. These men used private armies to terrorize hapless peasants into submission, and the situation in this case was made even more ironical by the fact that one of Bengal's Lt. Governors, John Peter Grant, had once praised Morrel as a model planter. Evidently, the Bengal government had failed to take notice of the gruesome tragedy affecting indigo peasants, brought to light in Deenabandhu Mitra's famous play, *Neel Durpan* (1860), almost a year before the outbreak of the Khulna disturbances. The rogues Morrel and Hely were finally brought to justice, and of the two, it is probably the latter who reappeared as the notorious Foster in the novel *Chandrashekhar.* Bankim was also aghast when men like these accused the administration of not extending adequate support and protection to them. This was a clear case of the oppressor masquerading as the victim. This reversal of roles was to become the subject of one of Bankim's essays, 'Bransonism'(1873).

For Bankim, the state prosecution of the notorious Khulna planters was important on two counts. In the first place, this demonstrated to him the powers of the state apparatus and of his own place within it. Bankim would have been only too aware of the fact that the official functions he discharged gave him and members of his class a dignity and status that they had to protect at all costs. An incident that occurred while he was at Behrampore (1873) fully vindicated such feelings. One afternoon, Bankim was crossing a field where Colonel Duffin and his friends were playing a game of cricket. Incensed at Bankim's not alighting from his palki to offer the ritual salaam to the *saheb*, the Colonel hurled abuse and physically assaulted the 'upstart' Indian. Bankim reacted by filing a criminal case against Duffin who was later forced to tender a public apology in court. Arguably, the Colonel's apology was directed not so much against the wronged citizen as at the assaulted public servant. Personal experiences also taught Bankim that not every offender could be similarly brought to justice, especially at a time when racial feelings among Europeans were high. Once, after being thrown out of a second class railway compartment by two drunken Englishmen, he advised all self-respecting Indians to travel first class. However, the Khulna episode also suggested to Bankim that the bad Englishman could be offset by the good.

During his altercation with the planters, Magistrate Beveridge was constantly by his side. H.A.D. Philips, the Magistrate at Burdwan, was a lifelong friend who also translated into English one of Bankim's novels, *Kapala Kundala*, and the Lt. Governor Sir Ashley Eden trusted Bankim enough to appoint Purna Chandra a Deputy Magistrate at his request.

Trouble over his official career was sometimes made insufferable by personal anguish and bereavement. Bankim lost his mother at the age of thirty-two and his father, about ten years later. One of his daughters, Utpal Kumari, committed suicide by consuming poison—a tragedy that Bankim re-enacted in the novel *Bishbriksha* where a woman similarly ends her life. His eldest grandson fell seriously ill (sometime in 1875), causing him great personal anguish, and one of his biographers notes how at the time, Bankim Chandra fervently prayed before the family deity at Kanthalpara for the child's speedy recovery. Around this time, family squabbles had reached their peak, forcing Bankim to move from his ancestral home to a rented house at Chinsura. The periodical *Bangadarshan* that he had launched in 1872 was now facing deep financial crisis. After running for nearly four years, the periodical had to be temporarily closed down in 1876. Unscrupulous press employees, the failure to recover arrears of subscriptions, and mounting pressure of official work all contributed to this situation. The following year, Bankim transferred the rights of the periodical to his brother Sanjib Chandra, though he still continued to write for it. For the next ten years or so, it was mainly Bankim's greatly popular novels appearing in serial form that helped the *Bangadarshan* to survive. In early 1884, together with his son-in-law, Rakhal Chandra Bandopadhyay, Bankim launched the periodical *Prochar,* which coincided with an important shift in ideology and agenda. The word *Prochar* in Bengali means 'propagation', and in the opinion of some critics, hereafter, Bankim's literary productions too came to be affected by tendentious propaganda.

During the period between 1881–3, barring a short stay at Jajpur (Orissa), Bankim was mostly stationed at Calcutta or in its close vicinity. Following this relocation, the *Bangadarshan* press too had to be shifted from Kanthalpara to Calcutta. It was here, at a rented house off Bowbazar Street, that Bankim first read out before his friends select portions of *Anandamath* that he was then writing. Not one of his friends uttered a word of praise even though they knew that he did not take criticism too well. Bankim's close friend, Akshay Chandra Sarkar, for a while, even took the word 'Santan' to be 'Santhal'. During the early months of 1882, he befriended the young poet Rabindranath Tagore who invited him to the family house at Jorasanko. Hereafter, the two appear to have met fairly regularly, though mostly at family gatherings or literary conferences. It is important to note that Bankim was among the first to acknowledge the young Tagore's poetic talents, notwithstanding some differences that later developed between the two. These differences were not so much with Rabindranath himself as with the Adi Brahmo Samaj associated with his father, Maharshi Debendranath Tagore.

In the early 1880s, Bankim became more widely known on account of the extended controversy (during September–October 1882) that he became embroiled in on the subject of Hindu idolatry with Rev. William Hastie, a teacher of the General Assembly's Institution, popularly known as Scottish Church College. On 23 September 1882, *The Statesman,* Calcutta, published a letter from Hastie condemning the hypocrisy of educated Hindus. In Hastie's view, the latter oscillated between an enlightened outlook upon life and superstition. The incident that provoked this outburst from Rev. Hastie was an elaborate *shradh* ceremony held at the Sobha Bazar family residence. Here, reportedly, several Western-educated Hindus, along with some 4,000 Brahman *adhyapak*s (scholars), respectfully sat through a grand ceremony which included the display of the family icon, Gopinathjee. For Hastie, this reverence shown to the idol only exposed the morally degenerate state of the Hindu mind and the 'defilement' of the Hindu soul. Two more letters written in the same vein appeared in the paper on 26 and 27 September, respectively. Bankim's first rejoinder to the Hastie letters, written under the pseudonym of 'Ram Chandra', appeared on 6 October. A regular exchange of letters followed, lasting until 18 November. Of all the letters that so appeared, one (dated 10 November 1882) was from Rev. Krishna Mohan Bandopadhyay, the Derozian-turned-

Protestant missionary, which first revealed the true identity of 'Ram Chandra'. Hastie himself, perhaps to further publicize his cause, brought out the entire correspondence in the form of a book titled *Hindoo Idolatry and English Enlightenment* (1882). *Prima facie*, such reactions look untypical of the man. It was Hastie who had once told his student Narendranath Dutta (the pre-monastic name of Vivekananda) that he would probably better understand nature mysticism in Wordsworth by watching mystical trances experienced by Sri Ramakrishna at Dakshineswar. By all accounts, this conversation never brought up the 'horrors' of Hindu idolatry even though Hastie would have certainly known of the saint's loving attachment to the goddess Kali. There is no evidence to indicate that the Bankim–Hastie controversy went beyond 1882; what we do know, however, is that the incident made Bankim Chandra more wary of Anglo-Protestantism, and strengthened his resolve to present before like-minded friends and companions, what he took to be 'authentic' Hinduism. Over time, this led to several major works like *Letters on Hinduism* (pre-1888), *Krishna Charitra*, and *Dharmatattwa*, and an unfinished commentary on the Gita. Importantly, the controversy also reinforced Bankim's scepticism about European perceptions of Indian religions and cultures. Bankim threw overboard his antagonist's claim that Sanskrit language and literature was better understood in Europe and America. On the contrary, true knowledge and understanding, he claimed, could arise only from empathy and an abiding faith in the subject. Hinduism, in this view, could be truly comprehended 'through a loving and reverential study' and only with a Hindu.

A relatively less known controversy was the one involving Bankim and the Adi Brahmo Samaj, one of the three factions within the Bengali Brahmo community. Socially and culturally, this was the most conservative of the three factions and was inactive even in politics. It distrusted the rival faction led by Keshab Chandra Sen for the latter's pronounced leaning towards Christianity. At the same time, it also disapproved of the other breakaway group called the Sadharan Brahmo Samaj for its support to both radical social reform and nationalist politics. At first sight, the Adi Samaj's strong adherence to the Hindu cultural tradition would appear to be fairly close to what Bankim

Chandra himself had been advocating. In truth, however, they differed sharply over conceptualizing 'authentic' Hinduism. Such differences are clearly manifested in Bankim's review (in 1873) of the well-known tract *Hindu Dharmer Shresthata* ('The Superiority of Hinduism') by the veteran Brahmo leader, Rajnarain Basu. Bankim's major complaint against Basu was that the latter had confused what was only an aspect of Hinduism with Hinduism itself. The adoration of the formless Brahman (Absolute) such as the Brahmos preached was indeed permissible within Hinduism but so were many other forms. Just as Calcutta was not India, Bankim added, Brahmoism alone did not represent Hinduism. In November 1884, such differences sharpened when Bankim contributed an essay for the newly launched periodical *Prochar* titled '*Adi Brahmo Samaj and Nabya Hindu Sampraday*' ('Adi Brahmo Samaj and the Neo Hindus'). This was a rejoinder to an essay authored by Rabindranath for the journal *Bharati*. In this essay, Tagore had accused Bankim of taking a rather utilitarian view of 'truth' whereby moral choices were primarily dictated by expediency. Bankim, in turn, felt that Tagore had failed to distinguish between the two possible renderings of the term '*satya*'—one as understood in the indigenous tradition and the other, derived from the West. Satya, in the indigenous tradition, was a term with several meanings whereas from a Western perspective, it was translated solely as truth/truthfulness. The latter was a mere translation of language, not of the idea. This propensity to fall back on meanings derived from the West, in Bankim's view, had destroyed all powers of original thinking among Indians.

At heart, the controversy with the Adi Samaj had little to do with semantics. Rather, it was symptomatic of a deeper schism that was developing within the Hindu cultural renaissance by the late nineteenth century. The foremost leader of the Samaj, Debendranath Tagore, was particularly disinclined to associate himself with Western ideology or keep the company of Europeans. This evidently ran counter to the labours of men like Bankim whose critique of Hindu society and religion were substantially influenced by their reading of the social and cultural theories of the contemporary West. In the late 1870s, such differences further widened as Bankim himself came to be particularly enthused by the writings of August Comte and the Positivist perceptions of Man. His critics, including members of the Adi Samaj, on the other hand, found godless Positivism to be utterly abhorrent. The irony here is that similar thoughts were also later expressed by Bankim.

In the *Sri Sri Ramakrishna Kathamrita* ('The Gospel of Ramakrishna'), a day-by-day account of Ramakrishna's religious life at Dakshineswar, there are interesting references to the saint's meetings with Bankim Chandra. This occurred in December 1884 at the Calcutta residence of the Deputy Magistrate, Adhar Lal Sen, a friend of Bankim referred to earlier. The conversation that followed between the two reveals the irreverently jocular side of Bankim. Thus, when Ramakrishna jokingly asked Bankim what had caused to 'bend' his body (in Bengali, the word 'bankim' means bent), the latter quipped that this had resulted from the kicks of the white master's boots! Again when asked to define man's basic objectives in life, he shocked everyone present, but more so Sri Ramakrishna himself, by suggesting that these were none other than 'eating, sleeping and sex life'. Yet another time, he ridiculed the institution of the Guru for, in his understanding, the Guru was the one who kept the choicest mangoes for himself and passed on the rotten fruit to his disciples. However, on his visits, Bankim is also known to have disagreed with Ramakrishna on certain important issues. First, he declined to agree with the view that a spiritual life could follow only from one's ability to overcome the temptations of material wealth. On the contrary, people who possessed wealth also had the option to spend it on a good cause. Secondly, while Ramakrishna believed that an understanding of the world followed from a knowledge of God Himself (If you knew the rich man, you also knew his assets), Bankim argued that an empirical knowledge of the world itself had to precede a higher spiritual life. In fact, one of his early essays had faulted the Hindus for paying greater attention to the life beyond than to life manifest in this world. Thirdly, and perhaps most tellingly, Sri Ramakrishna and Bankim disagreed on the conception of the god, Krishna. For Ramakrishna, Krishna and Radha were inseparable and virtually two aspects of the same divinity. Bankim, as we shall have occasion to see elsewhere in this book, was uncomfortable with the idea of a god implicated in a scandalous love life with a woman who was not his wife. But what Ramakrishna said seems to have touched him somewhere for the *Kathamrita* records that at the end of the meeting, Bankim left rather absent-mindedly, forgetting even to collect his chaddar on his way out. Incidentally, it also mentions how the English-educated 'Deputy' was awe-struck and possibly even humbled at the sight of the unlettered saint going into rapturous *samadhi.*

Bankim's writings on religion and culture never gained a great degree of popularity, mostly on account of the way in which he spoke of God and religion. All the same, they remain distinctive on several counts. In a later chapter, we shall examine how he took a dynamic and historical view of Hindusim. Alhough on the side of a Hindu cultural and religious revival, he deliberately stayed away from the more reactionary aspects of the movement. In the 1880s and 1890s, Hindu missionaries like Krishna Prosonno Sen (1849–1902) had created a strongly reactionary attitude against both Christianity and the West, which, at the time, did appeal to certain sections of people. 'The Christian's "God", when read backward, was only a canine creature' thundered Krishna Prosonno, 'not so the Hindu's "Nandanandana" (an epithet for Krishna)'. Around the same time, another orthodox Hindu Pandit, Sasadhar Tarkachudamani (1851–1928) drew large audiences to his public lectures in Calcutta by offering pseudo-scientific theories proving the superiority of Hinduism. Bankim attended these lectures initially but soon expressed his deep differences with the views expressed by the Pandit.

It is not commonly known that Bankim Chandra was also the author of eleven essays on popular science, all of which appeared in his periodical *Bangadarshan*. These were collectively published in 1875 as *Vigyan Rahasya* ('The Wonders of Science'). He is also known to have actively encouraged The Indian Association for the Cultivation of Science, a body instituted by Dr Mahendra Lal Sarkar in 1876, the Bengal Social Science Association (founded in 1867), and the Asiatic Society of Bengal, of which he was a member during the period 1863–7. In 1885, he was made a member of the Calcutta University Senate and after retiring from service at the age of fifty-three, he actively involved himself with educational institutions like Society for the Training of Young Men, later renamed the University Training Institute. Few people would now recall that apart from his numerous novels and other works of non-fiction, Bankim Chandra also authored three textbooks. Two of these were on elementary English and the art of composition, and the third was an anthology of Bengali literature to be used as a guide for taking the entrance examination to the Calcutta University.

Outside Bengal, Bankim was felicitated only once. This event took place at Khusrau Bag, Allahabad, on 27 March 1887. Apparently, in his lifetime, Bankim's literary fame had not travelled very far.

# 3

# Bankim Chandra and the Birth of New Bengali Press and Literature

He (Bankim) was blamed for corrupting the purity of the Bengali tongue but the pure Bengali of the old poets could have expressed nothing but a conservative and unprogressive Bengal. We needed a language which could combine the strength, dignity or soft beauty of Sanskrit with the verve and vigour of the vernacular. ... Bankim divined our need and was inspired to meet it—he gave us a means by which the soul of Bengal could express itself to itself.

—Sri Aurobindo

The publication of *Durgeshnandini* was like a beacon across the Bengali literary skyline. ... At Calcutta and in Dacca, in the western parts of the country and the eastern, there was great rejoicing. The people of Bengal could sense that a new age had dawned upon them. Evidently, new sentiments, a new thinking and imagination based on the life and labours of Bankim Chandra had come to stay.

—Romesh Chandra Dutt (Translated)

Amongst the periodicals, *Bangadarshan* is the most practical, patriotic and humanitarian in spirit.

—Government Report on Bengali Periodicals, 1880–1

Bankim Chandra once confided to a friend that writing in English came more naturally to him than writing in Bengali. Bankim's first novel, *Rajmohun's Wife* was written in English and serialized in the periodical *Indian Field.* It may also appear surprising that a man who was to be widely acclaimed for his contribution to the development of Bengali prose and as a major novelist in Bengali, began his literary life with a collection of Bengali poems (*Lalita O Manas,* 1856) that did not sell very well.

Bankim's early interest in poetry may be attributed to broadly two factors. First, there was his strong grounding in Sanskrit *kavya* (poetic literature) that he received at Kanthalpara. However, a stronger and more creative influence came from the contemporary Bengali poet and satirist, Iswar Chandra Gupta (1811–59). Bankim's earliest poetic compositions were first published in the *Sangbad Prabhakar,* a popular Bengali paper run by Iswar Gupta. Gupta was generally conservative in his views and preferred to employ older literary styles and standards. On the other hand, he was the major inspiration behind several talented writers and poets which included Bankim himself, the poet Rangalal Bandopadhyay (1827–87), and the dramatist, Deenabandhu Mitra. Bankim, however, soon gave up both poetry and fiction writing in English. Outside his official work, he hereafter used English for two specific purposes. To an extent, he used it for private correspondence with his more anglicized friends like Shambhu Chandra Mookerjee, editor of the *Mookerjee's Magazine* or the Positivist, Jogendra Chandra Ghosh. On the more creative side, he used it to review books, author a few essays (as for instance, for *The Calcutta Review*), and occasionally attempt full-length treatises. His 'Letters on Hinduism', a series of letters written to Jogendra Chandra, belongs to this category. On occasions, he was forced to put this to polemical use as during the public controversy with Rev. Hastie. His last public lectures on the subject of 'Vedic Literature' were also delivered in English.

By the 1860s, when Bankim Chandra began to establish himself as a major writer and novelist, the Bengali language and literature had already undergone several important developments. Some of these were mutually conflicting in nature and reflected deep-seated differences over cultural strategy. On the whole though, the issues that required critical attention were first, the question of bringing greater sophistication in syntax and structure, and second, literary enrichment through cross-cultural borrowing. For most of the nineteenth century, the latter was, by far, the more critical issue, especially in the face of new thoughts and ideologies coming from the West. This required a greater degree of adaptability and innovation. As Bankim repeatedly argued, new ideas required newer idioms of expression. For the Western-educated Bengali intelligentsia, this practically meant keeping away from both stylistically ornate Sanskrit prose and poetry, and the colloquialism of commonly spoken Bengali. The former was inept for carrying out new social tasks and the latter was found to be unsuitable for further developing newly acquired tastes.

In keeping with the established tradition, prose easily became the primary mode of social and theological disputes in the nineteenth century. However, the prose of the early Bengali reformers like Raja Rammohun Roy was palpably different from that of contemporary Sanskritists like Pandit Mritunjoy Vidyalankar (d. 1819), one of Rammohun's chief antagonists. In his several tracts addressed to his critics, most of whom belonged to the traditional literati, Rammohun pleaded for using a simpler language, a language 'closer to the people' by which of course, he meant people belonging to his class. For Bankim too, the word 'educated' meant essentially, the Western-educated classes.

The prose of Rammohun was certainly more elegant and intelligible without also being entirely free of conventional styles and forms of expression. In his days, the depth or dignity of a language was still ultimately measured in relation to classical Sanskrit. For the next thirty years, Bengali prose struggled to shed its Sanskritic bias. Even with the educationist Vidyasagar, there remained a distinct leaning towards *sadhubhasha*, the formal language used by scribes and scholars as against the *chalitbhasha*, the language of everyday use. Published in the 1860s, Bankim's path-breaking novel *Durgeshnandini*, reveals some borrowing from Sanskrit but this pleased neither the purist who found fault with its grammar nor his Western-educated friends and admirers who disliked the synthetic fusion of Bengali and Sanskrit. Such caution and conservatism notwithstanding, there was a growing inclination on the part of the newly educated to increasingly adopt Western literary norms and standards. Rammohun found fault with his opponents not only for their difficult prose but also for the lack of literary decorum. The Pandits, he observed, had the unpleasant habit of getting too personal with their criticism. In the opinion of some, Rammohun was also the first to use punctuation marks in his Bengali prose and create a distinct style in Bengali journalism. Another development that contributed to the growth of Bengali literature was 'translation literature', whereby selected works in English were either adapted or translated into Bengali. In Bengal, Shakespeare was perhaps the most translated author. His *Romeo and Juliet* was translated by Gurudas Hazra and *The Comedy of Errors* by Vidyasagar himself. Walter Scott and Shakespeare are said to have made an impact on Bankim's early novels like *Durgeshnandini* and *Kapala Kundala* while his *Rajani* is clearly modelled on Lytton's *The Last Days of Pompei* and Wilkie Collins' *The Woman in White.*

Comparable changes were also occurring in Bengali poetry. One of Bengal's greatest poets, Madhusudan Dutt (1824–73) had profound knowledge of classical Greek and Latin literature and was innovative enough to experiment with blank verse (in the well-known work *Meghnad Bodh Kavya* ['The Slaying of Meghnad'], 1861) and the sonnet in Bengali poetry. Rangalal Bandopadhyay increasingly moved away from the older poetic style of Iswar Gupta to new Romantic poetry, the best example of which was the *Padmini Upakhyan* (The Saga of Queen Padmini, 1858).

On the whole then, literary tastes in the pre-Bankim era were marked by conflicting loyalties. The orthodox readers resented innovations in language and the expression of new literary concerns; many Western-educated Bengalis, on the other hand, lacked the capacity to appreciate the new developments taking place in Bengali. Madhusudan Dutt was equally contemptuous of the Sanskritists and the culturally alienated modern Bengalis. The former he called 'barren rascals', but the latter seem to have shocked him even more. 'The poor devils don't know enough Bengali to understand what they read', the poet lamented.

The novel, in India, was adopted from the West and throughout the nineteenth century, the Western-educated middle classes, especially in the three Presidencies of Bombay, Calcutta, and Madras, were known to experiment with this new literary form. In the case of Bengal, there are conflicting claims about identifying the first novel. Some scholars feel that this honour goes to *Phulmani O Karunar Bibaran* (1852) by an English woman, Hana Catherine Mullens. It was shown to have the sort of domestic episodes that came to be identified with European works of fiction. For a non-Indian, Mullens reveals a surprising command over Bengali, and her work was, in fact, recommended for use in several schools of the time. At the same time, in its intentions, the work comes close to a tract or pamphlet whose overarching purpose was to propagate an idea. In this instance, Mullens used the work to demonstrate the superiority of Christianity.

The man more commonly taken to be the first novelist in Bengali, Peary Chand Mitra (1814–83), was a product of Hindu College. Peary Chand (pseudonym, Tekchand Thakur) wrote of a society where the infusion of wealth had contributed to visibly lower moral standards. His *Alaler Ghare Dulal* (1858), later translated into English as *The Spoilt Child,* narrates the misadventures of a rich landowner's son who is dragged into a life of debauchery by deceitful friends and sycophants. The distinctiveness of this work lies in its use of colloquial Bengali—the language commonly spoken by a cross-section of people in contemporary Calcutta. Bankim himself was to applaud Peary Chand for demonstrating how in creative literature, Bengalis did not necessarily have to fall back on the resources of either Sanskrit or the English language. Oddly, this is not an object lesson that he applies to his own fiction. Bankim seldom used the rustic Bengali language of the countryside or that spoken by the socially marginalized in the colonial city of Calcutta. When used, this is associated either with socially disreputed women or else to evoke a sense of humour. In most of Bankim Chandra's novels, there is a flattening of speech patterns. Thus, in *Rajani,* an uneducated girl, brought up as a flower-seller, speaks the language of a city-bred medical practitioner. In Bankim's view, apparently, the 'Alali' language (the language used in Peary Chand's novel) failed to separate genteel language from that which affronted upper-class tastes. From this followed cultural sanitization whereby seemingly 'vulgar' or 'obscene' language or that pandering to popular tastes was carefully weeded out. Bankim Chandra found both 'crudeness' and shocking eroticism in the works of the eighteenth century poet, Bharat Chandra Ray, in those of his own mentor, Iswar Chandra Gupta, and the numerous skits and farces that were at the time being produced in the Battala Press, the major publishing site of mid-nineteenth century Calcutta. Evidently, a somewhat puritanical and selective use of language was to be an important determinant of the new literature.

Bankim produced as many as fourteen novels in the Bengali language (and fifteen altogether if we were to include his solitary English novel, *Rajmohun's Wife*) over a period of some twenty years. His first Bengali novel, *Durgeshnandini*, was published in 1865 and his last, *Sitaram*, in 1887. However, Bankim also effected important changes in his works of fiction, sometimes adding considerably to their original length. From this perspective, the substantially enlarged edition of *Rajsingha* (1893), which is about four times its original size, has to be his last novel.

Of his novels, all but the first three, viz., *Durgeshnandini*, *Kapala Kundala*, and *Mrinalini* originally appeared in *Bangadarshan* and *Prochar*, contributing significantly to their journalistic success. Particularly in the case of *Bangadarshan*, the serialization of his greatly popular novels helped Bankim Chandra to tide over recurring financial problems. Some of these novels were translated into English and other Indian languages in the author's lifetime; Bankim himself succeeded in partly translating *Rajmohun's Wife* into Bengali, which was subsequently brought out as *Baribahini.* In terms of their narrative setting, only one (*Rajsingha*) of Bankim's novels was set outside the geographical limts of ethnic Bengal. Also, whereas several other works of his would also appear to be historical in character (as for example, *Mrinalini*, *Sitaram*, and *Anandamath* are), Bankim identified *Rajsingha* as his only historical novel. There is considerable historical material in the novels that Bankim chose not to call historical. *Mrinalini*, for example, was set against the backdrop of the Pathan conquest of Bengal, *Sitaram*, in the last quarter of the seventeenth century, and *Anandamath*, in the 1770s. On the face of it, this looks perplexing, and perhaps one reason for this is that in works other than *Rajsingha*, Bankim believed that he had used history only indirectly or that in such instances, history had not critically determined his characters. Posterity did not always agree with such views. During the swadeshi agitation in Bengal (1905–8), when a novel like the *Anandamath* became very popular, it was more natural to see patriotism as a continuous, long-standing sentiment, to somehow connect contemporary anti-British sentiments with those expressed by the sanyasi and fakir raiders of the late eighteenth century. In any case, historical fiction became a major literary genre following the publication of Bankim's *Durgeshnandini*. Protap Chandra Ghosh produced his *Bangadhip Parajay* (Part I) in 1869 and the economic historian, Romesh Chandra Dutt, four historical novels between 1874–9.

This brings us to the question of the popularity of Bankim's novels. Evidently, not all his novels enjoyed a comparable degree of popularity or commercial success. Works that brought him the greatest public acclaim or stayed popular over a long time were not necessarily his best, at least not when judged by purely literary or aesthetic standards. Thus, *Bishbriksha*, easily one of his finest works, underwent fewer reprints in Bankim's lifetime than did *Durgeshnandini*. *Krishna Kanter Will*, which many rate as Bankim's best work of fiction, never attained the popularity of *Anandamath*. But this is a point that ought not to be pushed far. Popular tastes change over time and sometimes, such changes are quickened by changes in the general social or historical environment over which neither the author nor the reader has much control. The popularity of *Anandamath* peaked only after a decade after its author had passed away and it was brought about, as many will no doubt know, by the outburst of Bengali patriotism following the Partition of Bengal in 1905. Besides, to judge the popularity of a novel merely by the number of reprints that it has undergone is methodologically a flawed exercise so long as we do not also know how many copies were printed each time.

When Bankim's Bengali novels are analysed, it is customary to classify them into three segments. Historians of modern Bengali literature suggest that the novels produced between the years

1865 and 1869 (including *Durgeshnandini, Kapala Kundala,* and *Mrinalini*) are characterized mainly by pure entertainment and aesthetic joy. In the second cluster of novels spanning the years 1873–93 (and including *Bishbriksha*, *Indira*, *Yugalanguriya*, *Chandrashekhar*, *Radharani*, *Rajani*, *Krishna Kanter Will,* and *Rajsingha*), this is somewhat overshadowed by moral didacticism. While the novels still retain their vastly entertaining qualities, they can also be found to carry undertones of social anxiety and moral caution. It is as though their author is now no longer content to reveal to us how the social drama in ordinary Hindu households unfold, but also how it ought to ideally unfold. In the third segment 1882–94, coinciding with the second period, come works that also carry didacticism but of a subtly different kind. We have already noted elsewhere how the novels produced during this period, viz., *Anandamath*, *Devi Chaudhurani*, and *Sitaram* attempt to bring about a potent fusion of patriotism and high (Hindu) philosophy. Thus, in both *Anandamath* and *Devi Chaudhurani,* a greater integration of the individual with the community rests on selflessness and self-disciplining, the essential idea of which is borrowed from a text like the Bhagavad Gita. Both these works make good tactical use of this classic text, either by inserting suitable excerpts from it at various places or (as in the case of the *Anandamath*, first edition) opening with an evocative verse from Canto XII in which the Lord exhorts man to work selflessly in this world but surrender the fruits thereof to Him. This cluster of novels, often called *Trayi* (The Three) in Bengali literary studies, also seem relatively less concerned with the pressing social issues of the day like widow marriage or multiple marriages in men on which incidentally, Bankim had a lot to say in novels like *Bishbriksha* and *Krishna Kanter Will* from an earlier period.

Allowing for some overlaps between the periods listed, this three-fold classification of Bankim's novels is an analytically useful method to follow. These help us to more easily locate the changes in narrative plots and shifting ideological concerns. In the following section, we examine in bare outline, the narrative content of two representative novels from each of the three segments identified.

## Bankim Chandra: Six Representative Novels

### *Enchanting Romance:* Durgeshnandini *and* Kapala Kundala

For a long time even after Bankim, *Durgeshnandini* was taken to be a historical romance. Some of its characters are indeed historical; on the other hand, it is not history but the play of human sensitivity and emotions that makes the work so distinctive. *Durgeshnandini* is a passionate love story between two pairs of individuals—Osman and Ayesha, and Jagat Singha and Tilottama. This, incidentally, is not a story where conflicting claims of love lead to violent retribution. Ayesha does not return Osman's love for her but yearns for the company of Jagat Singha. On the other hand, Jagat Singha loves Tilottama, not Ayesha. As compared to the complex narrative plot in some of Bankim's later novels, this looks remarkably uncluttered and straightforward. It emerges that Osman is by no means offended by Ayesha's partiality for Jagat Singha and even when they happen to be rivals in love, Ayesha and Tilottama are not drawn into any unpleasantness. On the contrary, once Jagat Singha and Tilottama are married, Ayesha turns into a person who is something of a cross between a recluse and a renunciate. The novel ends with Ayesha not only graciously retreating from the place where Jagat Singha and Tilottama are to spend their married life, but also selflessly gifts all her personal possessions, including highly priced gems and jewellery to the woman who has vanquished her in love. One might reasonably wonder if such a conclusion went down well with the majority of Bankim's female readers. Also, as far as the construction of characters goes, readers might indeed prefer Osman to Jagat Singha, and feel especially drawn to Ayesha's nobility of character. On the other hand, in Bankim's hands, Tilottama emerges as the prototype of the heroine in the new Bengali novel—young, extremely beautiful in appearance, uninhibited in love, and articulate.

There has been some controversy on whether *Durgeshnandini* is modelled on Walter Scott's historical novels. Bankim himself claimed that he had not read Scott before writing *Durgeshnandini*. In hindsight, this novel seems to bear greater resemblance to Bhudeb Mukhopadhyay's *Anguriya Binimoy* ('The Exchange of

Rings', 1857) in which there is an identical pairing of men and women. Thus, Jagat Singha and Ayesha are to *Durgeshnandini* what Shivaji and Roshanara are to *Anguriya Binimoy*. By the early years of the twentieth century, when communal tension between Hindus and Muslims had worsened, the idea of a Muslim woman's being romantically attracted to a Hindu man and that too unsuccessfully, was disliked by certain Bengali Muslim writers. In their view, the only corrective to this 'wrongdoing' was to have a Hindu woman being denied love by a Muslim man.

*Kapala Kundala*, Bankim's second novel, drew high praise from R.W. Frazer in his *Literary History of India* (1898) but even otherwise, it is considered as an extremely lyrical piece of work. The story in this case revolves around the fatal attraction that a young Brahman, Nabakumar, has for a woman of bewitching beauty, Kapala Kundala, whom he fortuitously discovers one day in the middle of a thick forest. Incidentally, the name Kapala Kundala is taken from the Sanskrit classic *Malatimadhav*, written by the poet-dramatist Bhavabhuti.

Kapala Kundala, abandoned by her parents, is brought up by a Kapalik (a practitioner of *Sakta-Tantra*) in natural surroundings, close to the sea. As it later emerges, the Kapalik had plans to involve her in certain highly esoteric practices requiring a female partner. Perhaps by revealing such intentions on the part of the Kapalik, Bankim may have tried to reiterate both the upper-class revulsion against such practices known to exist in radical Tantra sects as also to justify the Kapalik's ultimate defeat in his secret designs.

Kapala Kundala, though brought up freely in nature, is not quite comparable to Kalidas' Shakuntala for she seems to lack the tender and loving care of friends and peers. Also, she was never a part of a society through which an individual may be led to acquire certain social instincts and cultural values. Not surprisingly then, she ultimately turns out to be a failed heroine for, though married to Nabakumar, she has little clue as to what new social roles or psychological changes occur in a woman following marriage. Quite tragically, she is unable to return her husband's passionate love for her as she lacks the socialization that helps an individual express such feelings. In this novel, Kapala Kundala is indeed a somewhat cold, self-absorbed, and apathetic woman. She is, to cite an important example, quite unable to determine what constitutes human happiness. When probed on this question, she suggests that a casual walk by the sea-side gives her greater pleasure than the realization of commonplace social goals. Interestingly however, Bankim also infuses into her a certain quality of rebelliousness. At one place in the novel, for instance, Kapala Kundala strongly resents the sense of servitude that marriages seem to enforce in women.

After a series of dramatic twists and turns, the novel ends in the tragic deaths of both Kapala Kundala and Nabakumar. Both are drowned in the swirling waters of the Ganges though under slightly different circumstances. While Kapala Kundala voluntarily flings herself into the water, not knowing where her true happiness lies, her husband follows suit, not sure as to whether life would still be the same without the woman whose beauty he had always found to be so captivating.

*Kapala Kundala* has a point of similarity with *Durgeshnandini* inasmuch as this is not a story of fiercely contested love. It so happens that Nabakumar is married twice, but his first wife again never seems to cross the paths of the newly wedded. Certain other significant aspects to the novel are also worth recounting. Perhaps it is in this novel that Bankim first hints, albeit somewhat tacitly, at the indignities that Hindus allegedly had to put up with at the hands of Muslims. Nabakumar's first wife, for instance, though born a Hindu, has to convert to Islam along with other members of the family to avoid persecution. But more interestingly, there is a point of some sociological interest. Bankim is known to have asked a close friend, the dramatist Deenabandhu Mitra, as to whether a woman who is brought up in complete isolation from civilized society, would, upon entering that society, entirely forget her past. Reportedly, Bankim was not too pleased when his friend replied in the affirmative. Could it be then that Bankim Chandra believed that the institutions of civilized society tended to ruin the spontaneous relationship between man and nature? Here Kapala Kundala's rebelliousness and her sense of unease in society may only reflect Bankim's unexpressed reservations.

*Domestic Saga:* Bishbriksha *and* Krishna Kanter Will

*Bishbriksha* is said to bear close resemblance to the novel *Chandramukhir Upakhayan* (1855) by Rev. Lal Behari Dey though its popularity, judging from all accounts, was far greater. While reviewing this novel, the well-known contemporary journal, *The Calcutta Review* (1873) noted how it was to 'found in the *baithak-khana* of every babu throughout last year' and how 'while others (previous novels) were all historical, men and women, as they are and life as it is, is the motto of the present one'. Rabindranath Tagore was to later recall how with *Bishbriksha*, the story had turned into a saga and that what it revealed was within the everyday experiences of Bengali households. This novel, as one might remember, was the first to serially appear in the *Bangadarshan*. 'At the time, the *Bangadarshan* was the rage in Bengal', Tagore further recalled, 'and characters like Suryamukhi and Kundanandini (both from *Bishbriksha*) were seen to frequent many a Bengali household. The entire community was anxious to learn how they were or just what might happen to them in the future'.

The story in *Bishbriksha* is built around the traumatic experiences of three principal characters—a young and good-looking zamindar by the name of Nagendranath Dutta, his extremely beautiful wife, Suryamukhi, and another attractive woman by the name of Kundanandini. Unlike the novels that we have so far discussed, this one tends to equally reveal the evil, intolerant, and scheming side of human beings as also their honesty and nobility of character. Within the entire range of Bankim's novels, it also represents the first instance where intense romantic love and passion appear to be quite unmindful of social conventions. Thus, of the male characters, one (Nagendra) is drawn to extra-marital love and another (Debendra) tries every method to seduce a woman who is already another man's wife (Kunda).

Nagendranath meets the village girl, Kundanandini, on one of his private excursions and is at once drawn to her youth and beauty. What intensifies the mutual attraction between the two is that once Kunda loses her aged father, she is taken to Calcutta under Nagendra's care. Suryamukhi, getting wind of her husband's strong attraction for the village girl, has her married to her half-brother, Taracharan. This by no means discourages Nagendra, and as though to complicate matters, Taracharan's abrupt and untimely death turns Kundanandini into a widow and even more vulnerable to advances made by men. She now has a second suitor in the lecherous zamindar, Debendra, who tries to seduce her through the help of a female accomplice, Hira. This continues even after the widowed Kunda is married to Nagendra. Rumours about the private life of Kundanandini now assume scandalous proportions and Suryamukhi, unable to win back her husbands's affections, decides to leave home.

A parallel story now unfolds between Debendra and Hira. Hira develops an attraction for Debendra who does not return her feelings. This only makes her more determined to ruin the lives of those who she believes have conspired to ruin hers. From this point, the two stories take different trajectories. On the one hand, Nagendranath is increasingly forced to distinguish love from infatuation and to regret the injustice that he has cruelly inflicted on his wife. Towards the concluding part of the story, the two are happily reunited, leaving Kunda forsaken and all by herself in a morally precarious world. Unable to cope any more with this situation, she develops strong suicidal tendencies. A spiteful Hira takes Kundanandini to her tragic end by purposefully leaving a vial of poison close at hand. However, fate does not spare Debendra and Hira either; the first dies of grievous illness and the second, ultimately turns insane.

'The Poison Tree' (*Bishbriksha*) is a metaphor that Bankim effectively uses to morally caution men and women consumed by illicit passion. Such passion, if Bankim is to be believed, is like the seed from the 'Posion Tree' that can lead only to fatal consequences. *Bishbriksha* is notoriously conservative in its approach to man–woman relationships. The 'poisonous' effects of illicit passion are not mitigated even when such passion leads to marriage as in the case of Nagendra and Kundanandini. It is as though Bankim is trying to warn us that once drawn to the life of immoral acts, men and women are mostly unable to redeem themselves. But there are also other points of general interest. Illicit love and passion, we are told, grow from our inability to discipline ourselves. A man like Nagendra never had the opportunity to discipline himself for he had all along been able to obtain what he had coveted. To put it differently, the true worth of happiness comes only to those who have experienced unhappiness. Fatalism re-surfaces in this novel in subtle ways. Thus, even before she experiences trauma in her married life, Kundanandini has visions of her deceased mother warning her to stay away from Nagendra and Suryamukhi. That she was forewarned of her tragedy and yet remained powerless to prevent it was Kundanandini's fate. On the more positive side though, the author acknowledges the sublimating power of love and its capacity to visibly improve human life.

Two novels by Bankim, his very first (*Rajmohun's Wife*) and *Krishna Kanter Will,* hinge on family intrigue that is born of a disputed will. In the latter, a rich zamindar (Krishna Kanta Ray), displeased with the character or conduct of his own children, decides to leave behind a major part of his assets to his nephew, Govindalal. This is strongly contested by Hiralal, the eldest of his sons. Unable to persuade his father to change his mind, Hiralal leaves home and prepares to secretly replace the original will by a forged one. In this, he is ably assisted by two accomplices, Brahmananda and his widowed sister, Rohini. Subsequently, Rohini is overtaken by an acute sense of guilt and confesses her crime before Krishna Kanta. At this point, Govindalal intercedes on behalf of Rohini and prevails upon his uncle not to hand her over to the police. Following this incident, Govindalal and Rohini take a strong liking to one another, much to the discomfort and displeasure of both Krishna Kanta and Govindalal's wife, Bhramar. The former now changes his will yet another time, leaving behind half his properties to Bhramar. Greatly agitated at this, Govindalal refuses to put up any more with his wife and leaves home. Bhramar too feels that she has been unjustly treated and returns to her parents.

From here, events unfold rapidly and quite dramatically. Govindalal suspects Rohini of being unfaithful and fatally wounds her with a pistol shot. However, the prosecution fails to convict Govindalal for this crime as witness after witness turn hostile.

This, as we later gather, has all been pre-arranged by Govindalal's friends and close relatives and here, the novelist clearly uses the courtroom drama to point an accusing finger at the farcical judicial system put in place by the British. Two of the principal characters in this novel undergo significant changes over successive editions. Thus Rohini of the later editions is no longer as wicked as in the first and whereas in the first edition, Govindalal kills himself after shooting down Rohini, in later editions, he is seen to turn to a life of devotion and piety.

*Krishna Kanter Will* concludes on a note markedly different from *Bishbriksha*. For one, Govindalal and Bhramar are not re-united in the way Nagendra and Suryamukhi are. Bhramar dies even as her husband returns to her, partly out of her intense personal grief and the shocking news of Govindalal turning a murderer. In *Krishna Kanter Will*, the novelist's sympathy for the wronged wife and woman are more pronounced, and as a comparison of the two characters will reveal, Bhramar emerges as a more spirited woman than Suryamukhi. Thus, at the point when Govindalal is about to forsake her, this is what she has to say; 'Leave if you so wish and never come back again. If you want to desert me even though I am innocent, do so by all means. But do not forget that there is God above who watches us all. And bear in mind that one day, you shall have to weep for me, the woman you have wronged'. It is only apt to observe that such a voice from a woman and wife had probably not been heard before in Bengali fiction. It is rumoured that it is precisely to this spirit of dignified rebellion that orthodox Hindu society of the time took exception. If the extraordinarily beautiful and talented Suryamukhi could put her husband's interests before her own and bring about a reconciliation, they wondered, what right had Bhramar (who does not appear to be a very attractive woman) to abandon her home and husband out of a false sense of dignity?

The point of similarity in both these novels, however, is the fatal attraction that men and women often hold for each other. It cannot also be a coincidence that both stories involve women who have been widowed at some stage, thus raising the question of whether or not their second marriage was proper or auspicious.

### *Impassioned Nationalism:* Anandamath *and* Sitaram

Critics seldom praise *Anandamath* as a novel and its popularity with readers may be better explained by its exciting idealism than a gripping plot. One may also locate a certain paradox in the way this novel and the song 'Vande Mataram' that it included have been related to each other over time. On the one hand, surely, the attractive mother-symbolism of the song inspired many to turn to the novel. On the other hand, there is some reason to believe that it is the song that they found more inspiring than the novel. 'Vande Mataram' breathed life into *Anandamath* but also somewhat jeopardized its life purely as a novel.

While in some of Bankim's earlier novels like *Bishbriksha* and *Krishna Kanter Will*, it is human character that determines the play of events, in *Anandamath*, human character itself is shaped by changes in the external environment.

The narrative in *Anandamath* takes us through the adventures of a group of men who form the nucleus of a rebel army. The rebels call themselves '*Santan*s' or children though not in a purely literary sense. In a more meaningful way, claims to Santan-hood rest upon dedicating one's life to the service of the motherland. 'We do not recognize any other mother than the Mother Herself!', exclaims the Santan leader, Bhavananda. Here, apparently, there is a potent joining of several icons—the protective goddess (Mother), the land of one's birth, and bountiful nature that it represents. The Santans in *Anandamath* pledge to rescue this Mother from the abject poverty and political subjection to which she has been reduced by Yavans (aliens). While fulfilling this task, they are forced to clash with the combined forces of the Bengal Nawab and the English East India Company that extends military protection to the Nawab. The Santans do not also hesitate to intimidate their adversaries or loot money meant for the Nawab's treasury. On the contrary, such money is used by the Santans to arm themselves better for a decisive battle with the Yavan oppressors.

Into this larger narrative are included the more personal experiences of two couples, Mahendra and Kalyani, and Jibananda and Santi. Of these, Jibananda is already an active rebel and Mahendra is expected to progressively become one. Both Jibananda and Mahendra are shown to be householders prior to their association with Santans. Ocassionally, this becomes a source of worry and weakness for the rebels. Jibananda's continuing attraction for Santi, and Mahendra's anxiety for his wife and daughter only weaken the Santans' resolve by taking their minds away from their avowed objective. As in other novels by Bankim, moral problems are also created by some men who experience romantic feelings towards another man's wife, as for instance, Bhavananda's towards Mahendra's wife, Kalyani. Perhaps it is in *Anandamath* that Bankim for the first time uses a metaphysical gloss to explain a man's sexual attraction for a woman. The phrase he uses here is '*maya-rajju*' or the ties of maya. In high Hinduism, the metaphysical concept of Maya represents world delusion, the embodiment of which is the Goddess. It is the Goddess (manifested in all women) that deludes men, and keeps them away from liberating Knowledge (*jnan*) by entrapping them in her overpowering beauty. From this, it follows that men cannot free themselves of this trap unless Maya (the Goddess Herself) comes to their aid. In *Anandamath,* it is the determination of women like Santi and Kalyani that ultimately helps their husbands overcome the recurring desire to return to *sansar* (everyday life of domesticity) that fall within the domain of Maya. In the case of Bhavananda, however, there is more sin than error and the only way out of it is *prayaschitta* (an act of expiation)—giving up one's life in the battlefield.

In Bankim's conception, Santan resistance has some mass appeal, for, in one of the several encounters with the Yavanas, they are shown to have the support of no less than ten thousand men. The unity and single-mindedness of the Santans lead them to successive victories against the Muslims and the English, and yet in the end, these cannot be converted into something more tangible such as the establishment of a new Hindu kingdom. After a final encounter that results in heavy casualties on both sides, a mysterious Guru-like figure (the Physician) advises Satyananda, the leader of the Santans, not to take his mission any further. Pragmatism now demands that the Santans lay down their arms as an independent Hindu kingdom is no longer necessary. The country, the Physician points out, is progressively coming under the rule of the English and this in itself gurantees the return of peace and prosperity. Above all, this clears the way for the restoration of 'sanatan dharma', the eternally just order.

The conclusion in *Anandamath* appears to be in consonance with the arguement, often articulated in the contemporary Bengali press, that Hindus, in their own self-interest put the British into the position of power. In hindsight, it can be said that apart from leading to self-glorification, this argument also had the advantage of cleverly concealing the fact that in several instances, Hindu resistance had also been quashed by the superior military power of the British. The novel, on the whole, does not favour a violent political revolution but a peaceful and progressive transfer of power in favour of those capable of better governance. Some critics have consistently believed that in *Anandamath*, Bankim's conclusion was an apologetic back-tracking by a civil servant scared of offending his English superiors. Such an assessment does scant justice to the man and the patriot. It might be more justifiably said that Bankim genuinely believed in what he said. He did believe, for instance, that Indians were, as yet, quite unprepared to accept the responsibilities of power, and that this would come about only when they had brought themselves up to a level comparable to that of their rulers. Importantly, this is not an argument unique to the *Anandamath,* for it had been fairly explicitly stated even earlier. Through the conclusion that he gives to the novel, Bankim also puts forth the belief that an immoral act can never produce morally enduring results. The Physician in *Anandamath* strongly disapproved of the fact that Satyananda had turned to petty dacoities and armed violence in the pursuit of his noble objectives.

The novel *Sitaram* narrates the life and political adventures of a Hindu aristocrat by that name. Circumstances push Sitaram to an extended conflict with state power in Mughal Bengal, and the provocation, significantly enough, is the unjust treatment of Hindus by Muslim officials. Gangaram, a local Hindu, has been sentenced to death, allegedly for showing disrespect to a fakir. At this point, Sree, Gangaram's sister, prevails upon Sitaram to intercede on behalf of her brother. Sree feels that as a Hindu, it was Sitaram's first duty to rescue a fellow Hindu. 'If a Hindu will not rescue a fellow-Hindu', she asks, 'who else will?' Impressed both by this stirring appeal and by the personal charm of Sree herself, Sitaram tries every method to get the local *kazi* to spare the life of Gangaram. He first offers his entire personal wealth in return for Gangaram's life. When this fails to get the officials to change their minds, Sitaram prepares to take the death sentence upon himself so that the other man may be spared. The kazi, it would seem, is not averse to the idea of accepting the tempting bribe but cannot alter the judgement under pressure from the unrelenting fakir. In the meantime, a good number of Hindus who have been watching the proceedings get agitated and attack the soldiers escorting the kazi. The attack is successfully led by Sitaram and Sree. The latter in particular keeps inciting the Hindus gathered with shrill cries of 'Kill! Kill all the Muslims!'

After the state forces are driven out of the area, Sitaram goes on to establish an independent Hindu kingdom with the scholar, Chandrachud Thakur as his chief counsellor. Initially, Sitaram proves to be a tactful and far-sighted administrator. Thus, in order to escape being branded a rebel, he at once accepts the overlordship of the ruler at Delhi. On the advice of a fakir (Chand Shah), he gives the name 'Mohammadpur' to his new Kingdom so that this might foster greater Hindu–Muslim goodwill. However, over time, opposition to Sitaram and to his newly-founded kingdom builds up in many quarters. Quite irritatingly, it surfaces in one of his wives (Sitaram is married to three wives), Rama, who has frightening visions of a Mughal army violently over-running the kingdom. This is not an unrealistic fear, for, in the meantime, the local *faujdar* prepares to teach the Hindu upstart a lesson. From this point, the story takes a dramatic turn as, to put it in the novelist's own words, Sitaram changes from a *lokavatsal*, a ruler who has his people's interests at heart, to an *atmavatsal*, a man who thinks only of himself. There comes a time when Sitaram meets with non-cooperation and resistance from his own family members. Rama tries to get Sitaram to surrender before the enemy forces; Jayanti, another wife of Sitaram, withdraws from the royal palace and takes to the life of an ascetic, and even Sree, for whom he has developed a strong attraction, rejects his advances. Such resistance considerably affects the personal character of

Sitaram. Thus, in a fit of rage, he orders the public flogging of Jayanti and accuses Rama of being unchaste. At this, both Chand Shah Fakir and Chandrachud Thakur leave the kingdom, never to return again.

Mohammadpur is doomed when the faujdar, sensing that all is not well with Sitaram, amasses a huge army, recruited mostly from the North-west Provinces and Bihar, and in all likelihood, this is a cynical comment on the fighting abilites of the Bengalis. The faujdar's preparations prove to be on the right track as at the mere news of the advancing state forces, all but loyal (non-Bengali) Brahmans and Rajputs flee. Sitaram fights valiantly with God's name on his lips but clearly, even such bravery cannot undo the moral wrongs that he had inflicted on his own people.

At certain places in this novel, Bankim puts forth cultural arguments that are quite unrelated to the context. Thus, even when narrating events set in late Mughal India, the novelist accuses Hindus of taking to intellectual fashions that became common only by the mid-nineteenth century. 'They (Hindus) would rather read Swinburne than *Kumarsambhav*', the novelist complains, 'the writings of Mill, not the Bhagavad Gita and prefer European porcelains to the marvellous rock-cut sculpture in Orissa'. Here, apparently, Bankim was trying to locate contempory meanings in older occurrences, and detect failings common to Hindus across time. Although this novel appears to be about the moral shortcomings in men, it is also equally about the vision and sincerity that a ruler fails to bring into his administration. Sitaram's failing as a ruler started the day he put individual desires before issues of public welfare. A state has to be run with a vision and good measure of responsibility, warns Bankim. The kingdom of a ruler, like the chastity of a widow, he adds, can be kept intact only through a constant disciplining of the self.

## THE SOCIAL WORLD OF BANKIM'S NOVELS

An assumption often made in respect of Bankim Chandra's career as a novelist is that the purely aesthetic and romance-bound plots of his earlier novels increasingly gave way to intolerance and moral authoritarianism in his later works. Such assumptions need to be looked at more closely.

Historians of modern Bengali literature locate this transformation in Bankim by the early 1880s, when indeed he had turned to writing moral and religious treatises and brought greater idealism into his novels. It is also undeniable that greater social conservatism crept into his later works. Even in 1879, when reprinting some of his older essays as a book, *Samya* ('Egalitarianism'), Bankim deliberately left out passages that spoke of gender equality. His *Dharmatattwa* (1888) more categorically denied such equality. All the same, this turn towards conservatism was perhaps not as abrupt or dramatic as is usually believed. There were certain traditional perceptions about a woman's or wife's place in society that Bankim adhered to practically at every stage in his life. One of these was a strong disinclination to radically alter the status of girls or women. In the novel, *Indira* (1873), a certain character argues that those who advocated widow marriages, raising the marriageable age of girls, or educating the woman in a manner more befitting a man, had not the faintest idea as to the value one could socially attach to a wife's chastity and devotion. Suryamukhi, in *Bishbriksha*, can be heard to ridicule the efforts of the reformer, Vidyasagar, 'If he who authorizes the marriage of widows is a Pandit, who then is a fool!', she exclaims.

However, a moralizing tone may be found even earlier in *Mrinalini* (1869). In this novel, Bankim seeks to tell us not what romantic love between man and woman may attain but what it cannot. Thus, we have Hemchandra admonishing the errant female character, Manorama, in the following words:

> Love is as natural to human life as eating, sleeping or the pursuit of knowledge but certainly not as precious as the pursuit of one's dharma. A woman's greatest virtue lies in being faithful and therefore I say 'Conquer love!' ... Be careful Manorama ... human error grows out of passion ... error, in turn , leads to the neglect of one's duties and therefrom to the moral fall of the individual.
>
> (Translated from the original)

In the novel, *Chandrashekhar*, Shaibalini's infidelity makes even the stars shut their eyes in horror. In *Bishbriksha*, as noted earlier, the widow Kundanandini even when married to Nagendra, is forced to end her life once Nagendra and his first wife, Suryamukhi, realize their 'folly'—he for falling prey to carnal temptation, and she for failing to thwart her husband's second marriage. Here, the point to ponder upon is whether or not an entirely different conclusion was possible within the narrative plot of the novel. Also, one begins to wonder if Bankim's treatment of Kundanandini is more a disapproval of second marriages in men or women. Multiple marriages in men may be found in several of Bankim's novels—*Bishbriksha*, *Krishna Kanter Will*, *Kapala Kundala*, *Sitaram*, and *Devi Chaudhurani*, to name a few. On the other hand, a woman who has been so married is forced to meet with a gruesome fate. Apparently, Bankim took multiple marriages in men to be widely acceptable within the domestic economy of Bengal, and was even wary of any criticism on this account. Once, when an Oxford-based publisher approached him with a proposal to translate *Devi Chaudhurani* into English, Bankim politely turned him down, fearing that Brojeswar's marriage to three women would encourage the British press to cry hoarse about the 'polygamous habits' of the Hindus. At one place, Bankim's tacit support to such marriages is even placed within a Utilitarian mode of argument. 'While multiple marriages in men may be immoral', asks Nagendra in *Bishbriksha*, 'could we say that this will prove harmful in a majority of cases?'

Returning to the story of *Bishbriksha,* it might be justly added that Kundanandini's tragic end reflects Bankim's consistent opposition to the idea of widow re-marriages among upper-caste Hindus. The essay *Samya* claims that a (Hindu) widow who was chaste and loved her deceased husband would be loathe to remarry. Implicitly, this implies that a widow who did marry a second time had to be both unloving and unchaste.

In his novels, Bankim also brought out the unsavoury side to social reformism. In *Krishna Kanter Will*, Hiralal threatens to marry a widow to force his father to give him a greater share in the ancestral property. In *Bishbrisksha*, there is the instance of Pandit Sarvabhaum who can be made to sign a petition both for and against woman-related reform by the offer of money. In some other cases, reform amounts only to an outrageous defiance of social conventions and the tendency to bend public opinion through the use of one's personal wealth or power. This appears to be the case with Pashupati (in *Mrinalini*) and Nagendra (in *Bishbriksha*). Bankim justly critiques an over-reliance on Shastras (or scriptures) for effecting social reform, suggesting that this be replaced by a greater emphasis on public welfare or utility. On the other hand, he showed no particular enthusiasm for state-sponsored reform or for initiatives taken by non-Hindus like Behramji Malabari related to critical questions like a morally and medically permissible age for sexual cohabitation, especially as it affected Indian women.

However, given his deep-seated romanticism and an artistic sensitivity towards objects of beauty, it would be uncharitable to call Bankim a die-hard conservative in respect of man–woman relationships. *Durgeshnandini* represents a courageous departure from the existing social norms insofar as it admits to pre-marital love between the sexes. And unlike most contemporaries, Bankim preferred to speak openly about the appeal and power of feminine beauty even when suggesting that it was this overpowering beauty that led to fatal conclusions. He spoke of the fragility of happiness but also of the sublimating power of love. Arguably, this romanticism and the love of the human form were derived mostly from a reading of European literature but Bankim preferred to take this to the level of extreme idealism. In *Durgeshnandini*, Jagat Singha knows Tilottama to be enchantingly beautiful merely by the sound of her voice. Similarly, in *Rajani*, the blind flower-seller can tell, merely on the basis of a casual touch, that the man she loves is strikingly handsome. Some of Bankim's female characters are well-educated. Radharani (in the novel by that name), as we have earlier noted, has a personal library; Tilottama (in *Durgeshnandini* ) can read Jaideb and Kalidas in the original, Prafulla (in *Devi Chaudhurani*) is instructed in the Vedanta, and Suryamukhi (in *Bishbriksha*) learns English from a European governess.

On the whole, Bankim's construction of female characters was superior to that of the male. For one, the former appear more courageous in meeting their fate. Apparently, no female character from Bankim's novels who indulges in clandestine love lives long enough to reflect on her deeds. The men on the contrary, are able to do so either through pointless acts of heroism

(Protap and Sitaram in the novels *Chandrashekhar* and *Sitaram*, respectively) or by turning into idling ascetics as do Govindalal in *Krishna Kanter Will* and Amarnath in *Rajani*. Also, one cannot overlook how even when upholding traditional prescriptions about a woman's designated place in society, Bankim Chandra is quick to condemn any unjust acts perpetrated on her. Thus, in *Devi Chaudhurani*, even after his father forces him to desert his wife, Prafulla, Brojeswar is made to realize that there are few things as precious as a good wife. In *Krishna Kanter Will* too, the novelist is on the side of the wronged woman, Bhramar, who has the courage to say that her respect for her husband (Govindalal) would be in place only so long as he was worthy of that respect. In his day, it was perhaps Bankim, more than any fellow writer of his generation who asserted that the woman and wife were objects of respect.

Apart from the objections raised by orthodox Pandits that Bankim ignored, broadly two kinds of criticism were levelled against his novels. Tagore felt that Bankim's characters barely resembled the ordinary men and women found in contemporary Bengali society. Critics were also quick to point out how the Santans in *Anandamath* were modelled more on Protestant monks than Hindu sanyasis even though they wear the *gerua*. The contemporary writer, Taraknath Gangopadhyay wrote scornfully of how, in Bankim's novels, a Mughal princess could be heard to speak the language of the female graduate. The more conservative of his friends and admirers found a surfeit of romance in Bankim's novels. Here was an author who excelled in depicting the bewitchingly romantic relationship between man and woman but utterly failed when it came to presenting them in different social roles—that of a father, brother, sister, or mother. Incidentally, only two female characters from Bankim's novels—Kalyani in *Anandamath* and Kamalmani in *Bishbriksha* come anywhere near displaying *batsalya*, a mother's love for the child. Such criticism is not entirely misplaced. There is indeed an idealism in Bankim's characters that transcends everyday life. On the other hand, it would be just as fair to say that Bankim's primary aim was to develop a greater public interest in the new literature, not impart an earthy realism into his fiction. That realism was not altogether missing from his novels can be proven with reference to both *Rajmohun's Wife* and *Krishna Kanter Will*. The former too is a story born of domestic intrigue, and reportedly based on the first-hand experiences gained by Bankim when he was serving as Deputy Magistrate at Jessore and at Khulna. It is in this novel that we first learn of two new institutions that developed in contemporary society—the practice of bequeathing property by executing a will and the transportation of criminals to penal settlements.

## New Strides in Bengali Journalism

Bankim was actively associated with two Bengali periodicals, the *Bangadarshan* and the *Prochar*, both of which he had founded. Allowing for a few exceptions, all his novels, essays, reviews, and miscellaneous writings now included in the *Bankim Rachanabali* ('The Collected Works of Bankim Chandra') originally appeared in these periodicals. Especially in respect to the *Bangadarshan,* he was both editor and a major contributor. Over the years, meeting such responsibilities outside his demanding official work badly affected his health.

It would appear as though Bankim Chandra was quite careful about just which individuals or journals to associate with for other than the ones mentioned above, his Bengali non-fiction appears only in three other journals. Of these, *Nabajeebon* and *Sadharani* had been started by his close friend and literary companion, Akshay Chandra Sarkar. The third, *Bhramar,* was under the care of his elder brother, Sanjib Chandra. In part, this may be attributed to the hostility he often had to face from the world of Bengali journalism outside his own. Apparently, Bankim offended many by his unconcealed criticism of contemporary literary production. He once contemptuously compared the rapid proliferation of the Bengali press to the breeding of bed-bugs. In 1873, when a local daily, *Halishahar Patrika,* prominently flashed news of his 'grievous ill-health', Bankim suspected it of deliberately fuelling speculations about his imminent death. This, he wrote with some bitterness, was evidence of a man being punished for his literary opinion. Bankim Chandra, as his friend Akshay Sarkar once put it, was a literary rose on a thorny stem!

Bankim's earliest pronouncements on the need to evolve new standards in Bengali journalism appear in a public speech he delivered before the Social Science Association on 28 February 1870, which was later published as 'A Popular Literature for Bengal'. Here he complains about the social and cultural divide that was widening between the Western-educated middle classes who articulated their thoughts in English and berated the use of Bengali, and the products of vernacular schools for whom, the unfamiliarity with the English language was proving to be a major handicap. Another essay of 1878 ('*Lokshiksha*' ['Mass Education']) laments the neglect of mass education, largely brought about by the preferential treatment given to English medium institutions. However, such concerns go back a long time. In a letter in March 1872, that is, barely a month before the launching of *Bangadarshan*, Bankim wrote of the need to 'disanglicize themselves ... to speak to the masses in the language which they understand'. This, as he notes elsewhere, was a moral obligation dictated by *deshbatsalya*, love of one's country. Here what needs to be reiterated is Bankim's concern over both content and form. At one level, surely, attaining greater sophistication in language was an end in itself. However, this was also tied to the larger objective of disseminating knowledge—something that indigenous systems had failed to cultivate. In Bankim's view, therefore, what journals like the *Bangadarshan* would have to aim at was the 'filtration' of such practically-useful knowledge—knowledge largely acquired from the cultural resources of the West but expressed in commonly intelligible language. As early as 1872, Bankim argued how this would be especially important for women in whom unfamiliarity with English denied them information on major developments occurring all around them. It is quite apparent that when speaking of the 'masses', Bankim referred not so much to the labouring population in rural areas or in towns as to men and women drawn from certain classes. The *Bangadarshan* hardly deserves to be called an organ of mass education. Its more prominent and prolific contributors—Deenabandhu Mitra, Hem Chandra Bandopadhyay, Jagadish Nath Ray, Tara Prasad Chattopadhyay, Krishna Kamal Bhattacharya, Ram Das Sen, Akshay Sarkar, and Bankim Chandra himself, were all Western-educated, middle class professionals. The issues they discussed or debated in the journal were also typical of this class. By all available accounts, Bankim Chandra was not particularly in favour of introducing cheaply priced literature and defended his position by arguing that not everything ought to be made available to everybody.

The *Bangadarshan*, of course, was an instant success with the new middle classes in Calcutta and its immediate neighbourhood. In Tagore's words, 'it took the Bengali heart by storm'. Its impact on that generation is again best captured in Tagore's description, 'It was bad enough to have to wait till the next monthly number was out', he wrote in his *Reminiscences*, 'but to be kept waiting further till my elders had done with it was simply intolerable.' In 1872 itself, the journal had as many as a thousand subscribers and over the next four years, this figure rose to 1600. The annual subscription for the journal was fixed at Rs 3.

Scholarly opinion is unanimous on the point that in nineteenth century Bengal, it was the *Bangadarshan* that most effectively created public interest in the fields of history, archaeology, literature, politics, religion, art, and aesthetics. We have already referred to the eleven essays on popular science that Bankim himself contributed. These apart, he also produced three essays (in collaboration with Jagadish Nath Ray) on Indian music, and seven on the history and culture of the Bengali-speaking people. Other important pieces by Bankim were the witty skits or sketches that he subsequently compiled as the *Lokrahasya* (1874), the reflections of the opium-eating *Kamalakanto* (1875,1885) that many rate as his best work of non-fiction, and two essays of great sociological interest, *Bangadesher Krishak* ('The Peasantry of Bengal', 1872) and *Samya* ('Egalitarianism', 1877). A notable contribution that the *Bangadarshan* made as a journal was to the art of literary criticism. By his own admission, Bankim was quite selective in what he chose to review or discuss for his journal; on the other hand, on a rough count, he alone appears to have reviewed over a dozen works. These include the anonymous *Three Years in Europe*, a collection of letters, the well-known tract by Rajnarain Basu, *Hindu Dharmer Shresthata* ('The Superiority of Hinduism'), an anthology of old Vaishnava poems, *Prachin Kavya Sangraha*, edited by Akshay Sarkar, the neo-Puranic poem *Vritta Samhar* ('The Slaying of the Demon Vritta') by Hem Chandra Bandopadhyay, *Banglar Itihas* ('The History of Bengal') by Raj Krishna Mukhopadhyay, and the *Kalpataru*, a satirical work by Indranath Bandopadhyay. Evidently, Bankim retained his childhood interest in Sanskrit literature and when writing for the *Bangadarshan*, he tried to critically evaluate it in relation to modern vernacular poetry. Such questions surface in his critique of Bhavabhuti's *Uttara Ram Charita* and on the poetry of Kalidas (in his *Prakrito O Atiprokrito* ['The Natural and the Supernatural']). These apart, there is a critical piece on the medieval Vaishnava poets, Jaideb and Vidyapati, and one other that seeks to comparatively evaluate the literary creations of Shakespeare and Kalidas (*Shakuntala, Miranda O Desdemona* ['Shakuntala, Miranda and Desdemona']). Finally, a word about humour. Humour in Bankim is spread over many of his essays and novels, and to good effect. However, most of these occur in the *Lokrahasya*, a collection of essays that originally appeared in *Bangadarshan* between 1872 and 1873. Humour in these essays can be devastating in its incisiveness and the noteworthy point here is that Bankim is often persuaded to be bitingly sarcastic about his own class. Here is what he has to say about the educated Babu:

> He whose intelligence as a student lies trapped inside the covers of his textbook, as a young man in the wine bottle and in old age, in the comforting folds of the wife's sari is a Babu. ... He whose revered god is the Englishman, the spiritual master, the Brahmo, the vernacular newspaper, the Vedas and the pilgrim-site, the National Theatre, is the Babu ... He, who before the missionaries is a Christian, before Keshab Chandra a Brahmo, before his father a Hindu and before a Brahmin mendicant, an atheist, is a Babu ...
>
> (Translated from 'Babu')

At times though, it is only natural to take this humour as a subterfuge for an underlying conservatism. One of the most humorous sets of essays included in the *Lokrahasya* is called *Dampatya Dandabidhir Ain* ('Matrimonial Penal Code', 1873) wherein wives seek to legally define husbands as 'moving and movable property' so as to secure their own status and power. For some critics, this is more than innocent humour for it seems to fit in only too well with the thoughts and ideas expressed by Bankim at other places, both in works of fiction and non-fiction. Thus, in another essay ('*Byaghracharya O Brihallangul*', 1872), a wise member of the tiger fraternity sombrely observes before a gathering of tigers, 'Men are by nature weak and servile, every man needs a master who he wishes to serve and hence they make a woman their master. This is marriage'. While this could be taken as pure jest, the same argument re-surfaces in the *Dharmatattwa*, a serious treatise produced in the late 1880s, where Bengali males are shown to have disgraced themselves by attaching themselves far too much to the family and wife.

For a journal that set new standards in journalism and contributed so significantly to the growth and development of the Bengali language, the *Bangadarshan* seems to have a fairly chequered history. Originally located in Bhavanipore, then a suburb of Calcutta, the *Bangadarshan* press had to be frequently shifted, first to Kanthalpara, Bankim's birthplace, and for a while, back to Calcutta. It also ceased publication a few times and underwent a frequent change of editors. The journal was discontinued for the first time in 1876 when Bankim gave up both its editorship and proprietory rights. It was revived the following year under the supervision of Sanjib Chandra and ran successfully for the next six years. In 1883, it ceased publication a second time and hereafter, all efforts to revive it proved futile. Shochondro Majumdar, its next editor and later a biographer of Bankim, could not continue publishing it beyond three months. The *Bangadarshan* re-appeared several years later in a new series under the editorship of Rabindranath Tagore.

Such instability and frequent change of fortunes may be attributed to several factors. The problems endemic to the world of contemporary Bengali journalism were recurring financial trouble and unscrupulous press employees. The former is largely explained by the mounting arrears of subscription and here, the *Bangadarshan* was no exception. This might partly explain why when starting the new journal *Prochar* in 1884, Bankim lowered the subscription rate to Re 1 per annum. It is also apparent that the increasing pressure of official work left less time and opportunity for Bankim to contribute to the journal on a sustained basis.

Relinquishing editorial responsibilities after 1876 would have no doubt eased some of this pressure, but this period, as one might recall, also coincided with family squabbles and Bankim's decision to leave Kanthalpara. It is probable that over time, he may also have had some difficulty in procuring regular contributions from other writers, especially given the fact that they received nothing by way of remuneration. And knowing Bankim, it might just as well be said that he was still careful and selective about what to publish in the *Bangadarshan*.

As has been noted earlier, by the early 1880s, Bankim's literary and cultural preferences perceptibly changed. By this time, he had already authored a few essays on Hindu religion and culture, and introduced new concepts like *anusilan*, the practical meanings of which we shall have the occasion to examine later in this book. In this instance, his mind seems to have been made up by his friend, Akshay Sarkar's launching the neo-Hindu journal *Nabajeebon* in 1884. Bankim promptly followed suit by starting the *Prochar* that was committed to the propagation of what Bankim at the time identified as satya, dharma, and ananda—terms and concepts obviously borrowed from an indigenous tradition but now put to somewhat different uses. His views on the social responsibilities of literature now underwent a perceptible change as is evident from an essay that he wrote in 1886 for *Prochar*. In the essay called '*Dharma O Sahitya*' ('Dharma and Literature'), Bankim took literature not to be an autonomous domain by itself but a stepping stone to the 'higher' concerns of dharma. This does represent a subtle change from what he had chosen to express at the time of launching the *Bangadarshan.*

Not surprisingly, the bulk of Bankim's writings on Hindu religion and culture appeared in the *Prochar* and the *Nabajeebon.* The *Krishna Charitra* that marks an important turning point in the modern reinterpretation of the Krishna legend was serialized in the *Prochar* during the period 1884–6. The essays that had appeared up to that point in time were published in a book titled *Krishna Charitra-Prothom Bhag* (Part I). Bankim, however, resumed writing on this theme for the *Prochar* and a fuller work was subsequently published in 1892. This enlarged version of the *Krishna Charitra* also happens to be Bankim's lengthiest work.

After 1886, there also appeared in the same journal, several essays by Bankim on the nature of Hinduism and on Vedic deities. Sajani Kanta Das, a historian of Bengali literature associated with the Bangiya Sahitya Parishat (Bengal Academy of Letters) subsequently put these together as a volume to which he gave the name *Debtattwa O Hindu Dharma* ('The Essence of Godhood and the Religion of the Hindus'). Around this time, Bankim Chandra also began to write a commentary on the Bhagavad Gita, which, however, he did not live to complete. His commentary up to Canto II of this work was published in the *Prochar* between July–August 1886 and February–March 1889. After Bankim's death in 1894, his jottings going up to verse 19 of Canto IV were discovered in manuscript form. These were posthumously published in 1902 by his grandson, Dibyendusundar Bandopadhyay.

The major work by Bankim Chandra to appear in the *Nabajeebon* was the *Dharmatattwa*. This was originally a series of essays serialized between 1884 and 1886, but like many of his other writings it was published as a book in 1888. Later in life, Bankim was to regret the fact that the *Dharmatattwa* was not published prior to the *Krishna Charitra* for in terms of his scheme, Krishna was but the embodiment of dharma, and hence, the critical re-interpretation of the Krishna legend should have ideally followed a work like the *Dharmatattwa* wherein dharma had been re-presented to the Hindus both in principle and in praxis.

It is only too easy in being led to believe that the Bankim of the later years was a sharp departure from the earlier Bankim. But as will emerge in the following chapter, works like the *Krishna Charitra* or the *Dharmatattwa* are not so much contributions to theology as a strategic joining of a political will to a culturally revitalized religion. Writing for the *Prochar* in 1885, Bankim exhorted fellow-writers and journalists to wield their pens for considerations of neither money nor fame but only so that they might best serve the interests of the Indian nation and of humanity at large. Towards the closing years of his life he turned down an offer of Rs 500 that a popular Bengali journal, the *Janmabhumi*, was willing to make in return for a novel. To the man making the offer, he simply said that he wrote only for pleasure and at the time, his attention was riveted on better things.

# 4

## *Redefining Religion in a Modern World*

Even in my adolescence, I used to ask myself the question 'What shall I do with this life? ... and having pondered over this question for a long time I have now come to the conclusion that turning all our faculties towards God is true *bhakti* and it is this bhakti that defines the quality of being human. ... You ask me wherefrom I found the answer to my query! How can you possibly realize in a day that which has taken me a lifetime to realize?

—Bankim Chandra Chattopadhyay (Translated from *Dharmatattwa*)

Bankim Babu includes love and reverence in religion but these feelings may be felt and practised as cold moral virtues, as mere duties, as discipline. It is not until they are kindled into the white heat of ecstasy that they become truly religious.

—N.N. Ghosh in *Indian Nation*, 16 April 1894

On the subject of religion, Bankim's writings, whether in the English language or in Bengali, appear to have two inter-related aspects. First, there are various reflections on the social functions and responsibilities of religion. From this there also follows a more specific critique of the religious life of the Hindus. Analytically, these become inseparable. The latter could not have arisen but for the former, whereas the former would have remained somewhat incomplete and infructuous had it not also led to the latter. In effect, Bankim saw religion both as an abstraction and as a tangible part of human life, though conditioned by local history and culture. On occasions, however, this joining of agendas left Bankim in some inconsistency and confusion. Thus, while he grants the possibility of a religion without the concept of a God, the thrust of his writings strongly points to theism and the idea of a personal God. Again, while he led us to believe that for the Hindu, a morally pure life was clearly separable from the religious, his *Krishna Charitra* also argues that moral ideals reach their perfection in God, not man. Finally, while he borrowed profusely from Positivist writings on religion as a socially ordering principle, he also ultimately rejected it as imperfect and incomplete as it did not accommodate the concept of God.

In the domain of religious thought too, it may be useful to identify a radical Bankim as against the more guarded and apologetic figure of later years. On the other hand, when stretched too far, this would obscure the underlying continuities in his thought. The tendency to measure religious thought and practice against notions of reason and utility never deserted Bankim even at a time when he began to grow somewhat sceptical of these. Later in this chapter, we shall try to take note of the way Bankim's treatises in the 1880s are often rooted in ideas expressed far earlier.

For over twenty years, from the early 1870s to the time of his death in 1894, Bankim was actively engaged in researching the history, culture, religion, and philosophy of the Hindus. Such researches, it is important to add, were deeply influenced by the reigning intellectual trends in contemporary Europe. His last major work, the *Dharmatattwa* (1888) freely cites many European authors and thinkers including Kant, Fichte, Seeley, Comte, Renan, and Spencer in support of his arguments. Evidently, cultural introspection did not make him culturally insular. Even when wary of European perspectives on India or Indians, Bankim Chandra clearly distanced himself from those who believed that a modern revitalization of Hinduism was possible by using only Hindu cultural resources.

By and large, the more radical face of Bankim on the subject of religion is again evident in the early 1870s. The three contributions that are of considerable interest here are 'The Confessions of a Young Bengal' and 'The Study of Hindu Philosophy' (essays appearing in the *Mookerjeee's Magazine* in December 1872 and May 1873, respectively) and a lecture delivered before The Bengal Social Science Association in 1869. The last reveals Bankim's interest in cultural anthropology, for here he systematically classifies Hindu festivals by their probable origin. Thus, some festivals are shown to have originated in myths, some in stellar motions, yet others in agrarian production cycles. The interesting and original conclusion that he was able to draw from this was that most Hindu festivals acquired their religious character at a relatively later date. At the same time, these essays also choose to reiterate certain important arguments already in circulation among the Western-educated. Like Rammohun Roy, Bankim comes down heavily on the Hindu's penchant for asceticism and abstruse philosophical speculation. In his time, Rammohun had used the resources within Anglo-Protestantism and the Hindu Tantra tradition to propagate an affirmative and this-worldly religion, and his ideal was the pious householder, 'Brahmanistha Grihastha'. Like Rammohun again, but perhaps more explicitly, he relates the Hindu's preoccupation with metaphysical abstractions and an after-life with the failure to master the world of nature. Practical experiment and observation, Bankim noted regretfully, were never the Hindus' strong points.

In the essays, there are also tacit hints about how the very bourgeois notions of 'comfort' and 'respectability', admittedly derived from a 'very English education', would eventually replace a regressive religion as the organizing principles of the society then taking shape. Something comparable had been suggested by Rammohun when he argued how in a changing world, religion would be expected to secure some 'political advantage and social comfort'. In neither Rammohun nor Bankim was the transformation of religion into something secular ever effected. On the contrary, they ended up only reaffirming the view that religion was the key to an understanding of Hindu culture and society. For both, apparently, a social and moral reformation was contingent on the religious. When a contemporary once approached Rammohun with the complaint that the young men of Calcutta were fast turning from deists into atheists, Rammohun is said to have retorted that next they could be expected to change into beasts! Effectively, both Rammohun and Bankim circumvent the notion of a wholly secular culture by posing instead the question of separating the 'authentic' in the Hindu's religious life from the 'unauthentic'. The former alone, they give us to believe, could function both as an ordering concept in society and as a spiritually elevating religion.

The 1872 essay ('Confessions') strikes a fairly radical note with its sharp denunciation of the 'semi-barbaric restriction on food', an old-fashioned emphasis on ascetic purity in life, and the unjust insistence on 'perpetual' widowhood. Roughly two years later, writing for the periodical *Bhramar*, Bankim also produced a critical rejoinder to a fellow writer trying to make out a case for Hindu idolatry. In hindsight, the arguments that Bankim uses in this instance would appear to have been anticipated both by radical Derozians as well as more conservative Bengalis. In early colonial Bengal, even members of the traditional Hindu intelligentsia are known to have readily granted the unity of Godhead and the symbolic nature of idolatrous worship. Thus Ramram Basu (1757–1813), perhaps the earliest writer of Bengali prose in the nineteenth century, opened his *Lipimala* (1802) with a prayer offered to the One Supreme Being. Rammohun Roy suspected all along that his orthodox opponents were just as aware as he was that idol worship was irrational but still chose to oppose him for wholly different reasons. In the 1840s, upper-caste society had been unhappy at the agnosticism of men like Akshay Kumar Dutt (1820–86). Dutt denied the possibility of God determining, in any way, the fruits of human enterprise and Maharshi Debendranath Tagore, who succeeded Rammohun as the leader of the Brahmo Samaj, was once shocked at the sight of close friends and co-workers putting the question of God's omnipotence to vote!

Evidently, Bankim Chandra's thoughts on religion, whether in investing it with new social functions or attacking irrationalities within contemporary Hinduism, were addressed to a specific class. We can take this to be a fully bilingual class, equally at home with the English language as with Bengali. In *Dharmatattwa*, Bankim left several long citations in English untranslated on the ground that this would be quite unnecessary for his readers. More importantly perhaps, this was a class that had grown sceptical about their inherited religion but still unwilling to substitute it by another. Bankim's writings on Hinduism fitted this class admirably for, while on the one hand, they reveal honest self-criticism, on the other, they were not over-defensive. In truth, they also show some cultural aggression, either by way of questioning certain postulates or practices within other religions, or else by raising the vision of a self-confident, pan-Indian Hinduism.

Bankim Chandra is generally taken to be strongly anti-Muslim; what escapes notice here is his near silence on Islam as a religion. And while he may have had an occasional word of praise for Englishmen, Bankim held a rather poor opinion about both Christ and Christianity. In the essay '*Dharma O Sahitya*', which we have referred to above, he takes the Christian's God to be a tyrant who demands love and obedience from men, and wreaks vengeance upon those who do not so oblige him. It is here that his differences with Rammohun emerge more sharply. Unlike Raja Rammohun Roy, Bankim at no stage explicitly admitted that error and 'untruth' were common to all religions. Also unlike him, he made no serious effort to study religions other than Hinduism. Bankim was, in fact, quite offended to find that some contemporary Christian tracts were cleverly appropriating Rammohun in their renewed attacks on Hindu religion. In both his critique of certain aspects of Christianity and in contesting missionary 'slander' upon Hinduism, Bankim Chandra comes closest to his near contemporary, Swami Vivekananda. The odd thing though is that he never mentions the Swami, not even after his grand missionary tours of America.

With regard to the religion of the Hindus, Bankim Chandra made two points of some significance. In the first place, anticipating views now well established in modern scholarship, he tells us how 'Hinduism' was but a common name, quite recently and synthetically applied, to diverse religious faiths. The term 'Hindu' itself, he admits, was unknown to pre-Mohammedan India, not to speak of a common religion for all Hindus. The second argument, closely related to the first, rejects the idea of an unchanging religion, frozen in time. When taken together, such positions would cast some doubt over attempts to include Bankim among 'Hindu revivalists'. Rather than taking religion to be a fixed and immutable category, Bankim took a dynamic and historical view of the same, taking care to emphasize the elements of change alongside continuity. Surprisingly enough, for someone commonly included in this category, none of Bankim's novels are set against the backdrop of 'Hindu India'; rather they tend to be located in the more liminal stages in history when larger social or political crises tend to put human character to severe tests. Again, in his treatment of traditional Hindu philosophers or religious leaders, Bankim could be respectful but also forthright. When commenting on the Gita, he faulted both Acharya Sankar and Sridhar Swami, both greatly revered figures in the Hindu tradition, for having weakened the inner vitality of Hindu religion. His differences with Acharya Sankar incidentally, were not merely over scholarly interpretations but on the larger question of whether or not works dating back to the eighth and ninth centuries still had any contemporary relevance. Bankim's main objection here was that *Sankarabhasya* (Sankara's commentary on the Gita) was dated and quite irrelevant in the vastly altered circumstances of nineteenth century India. He states this quite categorically in his preface to his commentary on the Gita and even when commenting on the chosen *sloka*s (verses) of this text. From this, he drew the important conclusion that all traditions, not excepting the Hindu, had to be re-read and re-interpreted from time to time in keeping with the changing social and cultural necessities.

Blind obedience to authority, Bankim argued at several places, had led to the intellectual decline of Indians. Commenting on Sankhya, one of the oldest philosophical systems within Brahmanical Hinduism, Bankim noted with some disappointment how a philosophy that had the intellectual conviction to deny the existence of God, would not repudiate the authority of the Vedas. Almost until the closing years of his life, Bankim Chandra would not accept the Vedas as the basis of Hindu religious life. That these texts were of no practical relevance to modern Hinduism is an argument that he advances at several places, most explicitly in his rejoinders to Rev. Hastie and in the *Letters on Hinduism*. To an extent, however, this was typical of a Bengali

Hindu. Vedic learning and culture had traditionally been weak in Bengali-speaking areas, and even European researchers of the eighteenth and early nineteenth centuries had failed to procure a single manuscript copy of the Vedas in the province. In the 1840s and 1850s, under pressure from a group of young rationalists, Maharshi Debendranath sent a team of four Brahmo scholars to undertake the study of the Vedas at Kashi. On their return, the scholars declared that they had found the Vedas to speak with many voices from which the Samaj then somewhat hastily drew the conclusion that the Vedas could not be taken to be a revealed work. By the 1850s, the Maharshi, departing from the tradition set by Rammohun, replaced the Vedas with a new source book for the Brahmos, the *Brahmodharmagrantha*.

Bankim's reservations about the Vedas and Vedic culture have sometimes been over-emphasized. It has been suggested, for instance, that he did not take to Vedic and Vedantic philosophies because their 'quietist' and reflective modes of expression were unsuitable for his cultural self-assertion as a Hindu. Such assessments, however, do not stand up to facts. Notwithstanding what they might have represented earlier, both Vedic and Vedantic thought were to become the basis of an aggressive and culturally potent Hinduism in the nineteenth century itself. In upper India, this was the work of the Arya Samaj, and in Bengal itself, it was manifested through Swami Vivekananda. Besides, a decisive change in Bankim's attitude towards the Vedas came about in 1891–2. To an extent, this may have come about following criticism from people whose opinion he respected. During the Hastie controversy for instance, Rev. Krishna Mohan Bandopadhyay, himself a noted Indologist, had accused Bankim Chandra of being unduly disrespectful towards the Vedas. After this time, he seems to have developed a genuine scholarly interest in Vedic culture. The collection called *Debtattwa O Hindudharma* includes several original and insightful essays on the evolution of Vedic deities. By 1891, speaking to some students of Calcutta University, he claimed that the Vedas were 'nothing less than basis of our entire religious and social organisation'. One of his last but unfulfilled wishes was to write a novel set in the Vedic period.

His researches into Vedic literature and religion allowed Bankim to offer some interesting observations. For instance, it was his belief that the *mantras* of the Rig Vedas may have been composed but not compiled the earliest. He also sounds extremely sceptical of the 'heliomania' of European researchers whereby every Vedic legend, allegory, or poem is reduced to a solar myth. Bankim disagreed with scholars, both Indian and European, on the question of whether or not a certain verse of the *Rig Veda* (in the Xth Mandala) authorized the self-immolation of widows. While the belief, then gaining ground, was that such a verse had been cleverly interpolated by self-interested Brahmans (Pandita Ramabai, a scholar and reformer suggested this theory at the time), Bankim put this down to errors that had inadvertently crept in while the relevant manuscripts were being copied several times in succession. There is no reason to believe that through such arguments, Bankim was only trying to absolve a class of scribes and scholars of malefic intentions, for he generally subscribed to the theory that Hinduism had been increasingly vandalized by irrational accretions introduced precisely by such people. At the same time, he did also take the Brahman to be the source of all that was good and pure in Hinduism. The fault, therefore, had to lie not with a class as a whole but with individuals who departed from their rightful conduct and duty.

Much of the inspiration behind Bankim's researches grew out of his persistent disagreement with the substance of European scholarship on India. Thus, whereas even orthodox Pandits could hail Friedrich Max Mueller as a modern incarnation who had rescued the Vedas (as the god Vishnu in one of his incarnations was once believed to have done) and other religious texts of the Hindus from oblivion, Bankim found the man's errors to be as colossal as his scholarship. We may recall that even back in the 1870s, he had produced biting satires and hilarious pieces (in *Lokrahasya*) to demonstrate how a proper understanding of cultural texts and artifacts eluded most people. Thus, a newly-arrived English civilian could entirely misconstrue the narrative content of the Ramayana. Conversely, there was the case of the Indian *khansamah*, who, having watched his European employer say Grace when seated for dinner, was led to believe that the saheb was offering prayer to the food laid out on the table! The important conclusion he drew was that the texts and traditions of any culture were best studied with people who truly believed in them. On the question of Vedic studies, therefore, his advice to Indians was to check out the conclusions of Max Mueller with those of Indian scholars like Pandits Dayanand Saraswati and Satyavrata Samashrami (1846–1911).

### The New Possibilities of Dharma

Copious scholarly literature aleady exists on Bankim Chandra's innovative re-interpretation of the term 'dharma'. A German Indologist, Paul Hacker (1913–79), who studied his writings closely, calls this the 'most instructive instance of a re-interpretation of Hindu modernism'. Indeed, *Dharmatattwa* is not a conventional work on religion nor does it understand religion in the conventional sense of the term. Thus, whereas it does speak of God and of a religious life centred on Him, these are really part of a larger agenda which is aimed at securing greater social cohesion. Dharma in *Dharmatattwa* often acts like a regulatory mechanism that seeks to reconcile individual happiness with a continuing concern for the common good.

Several scholars following Hacker have argued that in this work, Bankim gives the term dharma, wholly uncharacteristic meanings—meanings that had no precedents in tradition. Allegedly, such deviation from convention followed from an attempt to graft upon an indigenous concept ideas that were both non-Indian and recent in origin. The noted scholar, Wilhelm Halbfass found Bankim's rendering of the term 'very Western'. Such scholars propose that while traditionally, the term was polyvocal and complex, Bankim reduced it to certain absurdly simple meanings and principles. It has been argued, for example, that with Bankim, dharma begins to be translated as religion. And though traditionally, the term dharma is always related to some context, Bankim tends to flatten the differences in contexts so that he could use the term normatively.

Scholars who advance such theories also tend to read Bankim's efforts as a part of a Hindu cultural reaction. Thus, his translation of the expression 'Hindu dharma' as 'Hindu religion' is taken to be a strategic rebuttal of the Evangelist claims of Christianity alone being the *satyadharma* (true or authentic religion). In hindsight, such criticism appears to be somewhat far-fetched, if not entirely misplaced.

In early Indian culture, the term 'dharma' had no rigidly defined boundaries and could accommodate multiple definitions and meanings. Hence, it could indicate the intrinsic quality in an object (as heat in fire), some moral imperative that could be applied to all societies (as for instance, *ahimsa* or non-injury), or duties specific to certain classes, castes, and communities (as for instance Kshatriya dharma or duties specific to the Kshatriya *jati*, or '*stri* dharma' or duties prescribed for a wife and woman). It can also be said that even in pre-modern India, the term 'dharma' could be taken to denote the religious identity of a people. In early medieval India for instance, Mecca and Medina are referred to as *dharmasthanam* (the site of religious worship) for Muslims. In early colonial India too, one of Rammohun's many opponents, Pandit Kashinath Tarkapanchanan, called himself *dharmasthapanarthi* or one keen to re-establish the authentic religious culture. That Pandit Kashinath used these terms in the sense of religion is evident from his accusing Rammohun of losing his Hindu identity by openly mixing with non-Hindus. Well before Bankim began translating the term dharma as religion, this use was in vogue within the world of Bengali journalism. Between the years 1840 and 1881, there were at least ten Bengali periodicals using dharma either as a prefix or suffix and also clearly taking the term to mean religion. The unique side to Bankim's work is not so much that it takes dharma to be analogous to religion but the tendency to transcend its context-determined character. In his writings, dharma does begin to denote duties specific to certain social classes or groups, but it is also used as an impersonal and abstract concept that is capable of transcending these specificities. This juxtaposition of meanings was important for Bankim for that was one of the ways in which he could integrate the *moksha*-centric individualism of the Hindu with a new emphasis on social cohesion that had gained ascendancy in the contemporary West.

By nature, *Dharmatattwa* is a difficult work, not easily reduced to simple ideas or precepts. All the same, its major arguments may be briefly summed up as follows:

1. It was a person's dharma (duty) to manifest qualities that defined a man (*manushatya*). This manushatya was the innate quality (dharma) of the person and could be realized through the disciplined cultivation (anusilan) of the various human faculties of the body and mind. These Bankim identifies as *gyanarjini*, *karyakarini*, *chittaranjini*, and *shararaki* (intellectual scrutiny, ethical conduct, aesthetic enjoyment, and development of the physical self).
2. It was important, however, for this task to be carried out in a manner that ruled out a disproportionate emphasis on any one of these faculties. The objective was to bring about *samnjasya* or the harmonious integration of all.
3. From this, it followed that it would be just as *dharmic* (morally and socially sound) to love oneself as to love mankind and God. It was the neglect of the self that accounted for the fact that the Hindu civilization was not progressing enough to keep pace with the developments occurring elsewhere in the world.
4. However, an enlightened self-interest or individual happiness had to be progressively made more sublime through universal love which would combine love of self, of one's family, of the country, and more generally, love and compassion for all forms of life. Happily, this task was facilitated by the omnipresence of God in His creation. Love of life and of God thus became interchangeable.
5. Anusilan itself reached its fullness when turned towards the adoration of God for He was the moral exemplar and the source of all spiritual life.

A critical assessment of *Dharmatattwa* and of its place in Bankim's thought would be incomplete without some reference to some of its more significant aspects. Predictably, the major conceptual categories employed in this work appeared as early as the 1870s. Thus the term 'anusilan' occurs in 1873 and in an essay of 1877–8, titled '*Manushatya Kee*' ('What is it to be human?'), where Bankim anticipates the major argument in *Dharmatattwa* by suggesting that the moral progress of an individual was directly proportional to his selflessness and sense of social duty. This tends to question the commonplace assumption that *Dharmatattwa* essentially grew out of Bankim's disagreements with Pandit Sashadhar's exposition of Hinduism in 1881–2. Disagreements with the Pandit may indeed have strengthened Bankim's resolve to present an alternative conception of Hindu dharma, not created yet. Secondly, while there is indeed a strong intellectual impact of the West on Bankim's work, one must not lose sight of the copious use he makes of Hindu religious texts, concepts, and categories. The idea of religion as the rallying point in society is admittedly un-Hindu and is borrowed primarily from Comte and Positivist theory. However, this is also suitably embellished by a fairly lengthy discourse on bhakti and nishkam karma (unmotivated action), both of which are distinctly Indian and Hindu in origin. In fact, what surprises one about *Dharmatattwa* is the facile way in which dharma, even as a socially regulatory concept, is so Hinduized in conception and character. At first sight, Bankim does appear to be oblivious of the non-Hindu.

However, in this work, bhakti itself has two faces, one of which is unrecognizable as Hindu. On the one hand, it speaks of the adoration of God, and on the other of the individual's obligation towards his community (*samaj*). Bankim was quite disappointed to find that people of his generation showed fear, not respect for society. As far as bhakti was related to the task of integrating the individual to the community, it also had to create a well-defined network of inter-personal relationships. Thereafter, it had to be employed in fortifying traditionally prescribed hierarchies whereby the pupil came to venerate the teacher, the lower castes, the Brahman, and the wife, her husband. In *Dharmatattwa*, nishkam karma too is deeply embedded in bhakti for selflessness helped to uphold one's social obligations or at least to bear their burden gracefully. Importantly though, the exemplar of such selflessness and compassion is not a figure from the pages of history but the mythical hero Prahlad. Even as a son of a demon-king, Prahlad exhibits unflinching bhakti for Vishnu (of whom Krishna was an avatar) and the exemplary virtues of forgiveness and thinking beyond the self. Here, the choice of Prahlad seems to fulfil two important needs within the argumentative framework of Bankim's works. First, it helps him to suitably supplement what could otherwise have been a wholly secular idea, with popular religious imagery. Prahlad furnishes Bankim with the opportunity to more emphatically bring out the intrinsic 'superiority' of Vaishnava bhakti. At the same time, it enables him to make the important point that the samaj and its constitutive elements were not independent of God. Love of God led to love and compassion for his creations; conversely, working selflessly in society was the surest way to attain God.

## BANKIM CHANDRA AND THE TURN TOWARDS NEO-PURANISM

It has often been suggested that the underlying message in Bankim's *Krishna Charitra* too is only thinly theological. In this view, Krishna was deliberately projected as the counterpoint to both Christ and the architects of the modern nation-states in Europe such as Napoleon, Cavour, and Bismarck. He was the political icon around whom the new Indian nation could take shape and a cultural symbol that could restore the self-belief of the Hindus.

At one level, surely, Krishna in the *Krishna Charitra* appears not so much as a god who elicits love and devotion as a synthetically constructed ideal for humanity to follow. This Krishna is constructed almost clinically; he is the embodiment of all moral virtues, an astute diplomat and statesman, and the exemplar of grace, equanimity, and forbearance, none of whose thought or actions could really be faulted. In other words, his life most aptly demonstrates just how or in what manner a dharmic life may be led. In this sense, *Krishna Charitra* is but the logical conclusion to the project that Bankim launched with *Dharmatattwa.* The latter talks of the virtues to be realized on this earth, the former of He who is supremely virtuous. Bankim, however, complicated matters by trying to establish Krishna both as an historical actor and God incarnate. Now if it was Bankim's wish to rescue a historical character from the layers of myths that had come to surround him, he might have well limited his project to an analytical separation of myth from history. In truth, however, he is no less eager to play upon the traditional idea of an avatar and establish it in history. Here, he also appears to overlook the fact that the sources primarily used in this enterprise, viz., the Puranas and the epics, were literary in character, not historical, though they did throw some light on the historical past.

Why then does Bankim mix up pragmatism with poetic ideals? A possible answer to this lies in his reluctance to admit the religious and the secular as two separate domains. A clue to this may be obtained from the remark he once made in his *Letters on Hinduism* on how with the Hindus, religion could never be expressed through a single word or term as it pervaded every aspect of their lives. With Bankim then, the non-religious was also an integral part of the religious for they were both within the domain created by God. Here it must be assumed that he was also influenced by the dominant trend of thinking in Victorian Britain that found secular work to be just as pleasing to God as the religious. In *Krishna Charitra* itself, this allowed the author to join reason and historical pragmatism to the deeply theological idea of *lila,* God's capricious play on earth. Here, we cannot but notice the fact that the concept of lila itself was typically Vaishnava in origin and post-Chaitanya Vaishnava poetry in Bengal had itself valourized Krishna's appearance as man (*nara-lila*) as the most sublime of his avataric forms much before Bankim chose to do so. The unique quality about *Krishna Charitra* then, was not so much the celebration of Krishna's descent on earth as man but in the emphasis that this could be understood as history.

There is a fairly serious academic side to this work that remains somewhat understated, particularly by those who get carried away by its polemical character. There is, for instance, a critical scrutiny of Puranic myths and fables, often ending in rather bold conclusions. In *Krishna Charitra*, for example, Bankim dismissed outright, the conception of avatars appearing in aquatic or animal forms such as the fish (*matsya*), the tortoise (*kurma*), a boar (*varaha*), or the bizarre man-lion (*Nrismha*). This was indeed an extraordinary position to take at a time when pseudo-scientific theoreticians of modern Hinduism were trying to draw parallels between the sequence of avatars and Darwinian evolutionary cycles. The other important side of this work is the rigorous textual scrutiny, particularly of the Mahabharata, which he took to be the most authentic and the oldest extant source on the life and work of Krishna. In his view, the Mahabharata as available in his day was a grossly dilated version of the original. Allegedly, this followed from continuous interpolation, whereby layer upon layer of irrational fables and myths was added to a core text by interested scholars and scribes.

Quite evidently, Bankim's researches on Mahabharata and other related sources on the life of Krishna only widened the gap between the two broad conceptions of this god in tradition. One of these was the wily statesman, implicated in the great war at Kurukshetra and to whom was attributed the sermon, Bhagavad Gita. The other was the pastoral, scandalously playful figure from Vrindavan, the subject of some of the finest Indian poetry. Understandably enough, Bankim refused to acknowledge the latter. The poets he accused of unduly eroticizing human sentiment and ascribing to God acts that would be highly reproachful even for ordinary men and women. There is a widely circulated story to the effect that even as a young boy at Kanthalpara, Bankim had shocked a local gathering with the remark that the deity that his family worshipped could not have been the god guilty of violating the modesty of woman. In *Krishna Charitra*, Bankim even refused to translate into Bengali, passages from the *Bhagavat Purana*, describing the well-known episode of Krishna's stealing the garments of women bathing in a nearby tank. He feared that when taken literally, such descriptions would particularly affect the moral character of women and children. Not surprisingly, Bankim Chandra disapproved of the sensuous poetry in Jaideb's *Gita Gobinda*, arguing that such poetry had only contributed to make Bengalis more effeminate and morally weak as a race. Here again, his views are strikingly similar to those of Vivekananda who found Vaishnava sentimentalism, expressed through kirtans or erotic love poetry, grossly detrimental to the recovery of manliness.

In *Krishna Charitra*, Bankim Chandra valorizes a god who was revered in neither folk life nor high textual culture. The author of the sermon at Kurukshetra, for instance, was not the god worshipped in wayside shrines and Hindu households. His refusal to admit the *Bhagavat Purana* as a reliable source on Krishna's life and exploits also isolated him from a powerful stream of high Vaishnava culture, which had, to its credit, very sophisticated works on religious literature, art, and aesthetics. Bankim's representation of Krishna, one imagines, would have looked even more unfamiliar to his contemporaries for its reluctance to acknowledge the god's widely celebrated consort, Radha. Here, obviously, Bankim and like-minded men of his generation were extremely uncomfortable with the fact that in some traditions Radha was another man's wife and in some others, his maternal aunt. Judged from such perspectives, the love life of Radha and Krishna was tainted with both adultery and incest. Obviously, Bankim did not subscribe to the theory advanced in Vaishnava *Rasa Shastra* (aesthetics) that such scandalous attraction between a man and woman was but an allegory for man's yearning for God. On the contrary, he was embarrassed to hear recurring criticism from Christian missionaries for whom a 'lecherous' god was but a reminder of the Hindu's moral depravity. Over time, however, Bankim's views on Radha and the *Bhagavat Purana* changed. The revised edition of *Krishna Charitra* admitted the *Bhagavat Purana* as a reliable source on the life of Krishna while also warning its readers not to take erotic descriptions literally.

*Krishna Charitra* claims to reveal only the human face of Krishna, not the divine. The reader is repeatedly told how, when in human form, God never revealed His divine origins or used His divine powers to overpower His opponents. Critics like Tagore, on the other hand, accused Bankim of taking this argument too far. Given the fact that the sources on the life of Krishna were essentially literary creations, it was unjust to treat as an interpolation anything that seemed out of the ordinary. Poetic creations, after all, were not constrained to talk only of ideal types. On the whole, it was Tagore's feeling that in *Krishna Charitra*, Bankim valorizes not God but man's powers of rational and independent thinking. This is indeed a fair assessment but for the fact that in this work as also in *Dharmatattwa*, there is a palpable leaning towards bhakti and the idea of a personal God. Several contemporaries relate this to Bankim's childhood love and reverence for the family deity. Even in adulthood, Bankim was deeply attached to this deity and prayed before it in times of personal distress. Cultural contestations may indeed constitute a powerful voice within *Krishna Charitra*, but hidden behind this, there also appears to have been a pulsating personal piety. Perhaps Bankim's problem essentially was not an utter inability to reveal a god that could be revered but the presumption that this could rest equally on personal faith and impersonal reason.

*Krishna Charitra* may justly be regarded as a neo-Puranic work inasmuch as it seeks to relocate within a new interpretative framework, a figure widely celebrated in the medieval Puranas. The concept of an avatar and of lila, categories which Bankim employs, albeit guardedly, are again Puranic in their origin and character. Works like *Dharmatattwa* and *Krishna Charitra* may, in fact, be said to have started a Puranic revival. It was the recovery of a religious culture that had been partly buried and marginalized by both Brahmo iconoclasm and the gradual advent of metaphysical Vedanta. This has persuaded some scholars to suggest that Bankim's Krishna-bhakti, however unique or outlandish it might have appeared to his contemporaries, was at heart a reaction to Rammohun's positive distaste for Vaishnavism and Puranic culture.

It is quite probable that Bankim Chandra's re-interpretation of the Krishna legend was influenced by comparable attempts made in Europe to historicize the life and work of Christ, and here, one can readily think of the critical scholarlship of thinkers like Renan and Strauss. On the other hand, a figure exactly comparable to Krishna would not have suited Bankim's agenda, which sought not an ascetic but a householder. Krishna was a better ideal than Christ as he was known to better combine in himself the responsibilities and functions of a man in this world. And though *Krishna Charitra* is a work of the older Bankim, we catch a fragment of his anxiety even in a work of 1872:

> Where is the man amongst us, who in personal purity, in meekness, in self-forgetfulness, in genuine, non-political patriotic feeling ... (in) systematic devotion to knowledge and virtue for their own sake, can stand a moment's comparison with the better order of minds nurtured in the cradle of Hinduism?

Apparently, Bankim Chandra found no man who could meet such requirements, whether from his own time or from the past. It is thus that he turned to a God, but a God who loved His creation and felt obliged to set worthy examples for man to follow.

# 5

# The Nation as Mother
## Bankim Chandra and Advancing Hindu Nationalism

Of the new spirit which is leading the nation to resurgence and independence, he [Bankim] was the inspirer and political guru.

—*Bande Mataram*, 16 April 2007

'Revolution', he [Bankim] wrote in his preface to the first edition of the *Anandamath*, 'are very generally processes of self-torture and rebels are suicides. The English have served Bengal from anarchy. These truths are elucidiated in this work'. It was a curious irony of fate, surely, that it should have been the very book that the revolutionaries should have been so deeply drawn for inspiration.

—Lord Ronaldshay, *The Heart of Aryavarta*

To most contemporary Indians, Bankim Chandra is primarily known as the author of the song 'Vande Mataram' ('I bow to thee, Mother') adopted by the Constituent Assembly as the National Song in 1951. A few may be even heard to (mistakenly) suggest that it was written for the patriotic novel, *Anandamath*. However, even in Bengal, not many know that Bankim's contribution to Indian nationalism was not so much by way of a virulent anti-British/anti-colonial sentiment as by making fellow Bengalis and generally, all Indians, more self-conscious as a people. In Bankim Chandra's political understanding, 'swaraj' would largely mean a positive self-awareness, a foundation upon which to rest one's true credibility and claims. A people without an awareness of what they had once achieved or were indeed capable of further achieving, would find it hard to get other people to acknowledge their claims. From this, it followed that a sense of history was a constitutive element of politics. People who had not historically commemorated their past would struggle to construct a modern nationhood. In this sense, Bankim Chandra was one of those who had come to believe that political freedom was meaningless without a people being first liberated socially and intellectually. Like Swami Vivekananda after him, Bankim Chandra seems to have rejected the political praxis, partly no doubt because of his status as a civil servant but also because he believed that the substance of political culture lay in the cultural self-discovery of a people.

Between 1872 and 1876, Bankim Chandra contributed as many as sixteen essays to the *Bangadarshan*, the purpose of which was to critically re-assess current theories or beliefs seeking to explain India's loss of freedom. Of these, as many as fourteen were on the social origins of Bengali Hindus as also their histories, literary accomplishments, religious lives, and culture. These also reveal a greater passion or intensity, and a fuller use of the historical and ethnographic material currently available. By comparison, the essays dealing with India as a whole such as '*Bharat Kalanka*' ('India Shamed'), and '*Bharatvasher Swadhinata O Paradhinata*' ('The Freedom and Subjection of India') are more general in nature. In the second of these essays, Bankim is even naïve enough to argue that in British India, the law made no operative distinction between the European and the Indian. This he took to be a radical improvement upon the *Smriti* law of the Hindus that enforced greater punishment on the Sudra than on the Brahman, even for the same offence. At first glance, this does sound strange for, as an administrator, Bankim should have known of the ways in which laws were often violated in favour of the ruling class and even non-official European settlers.

All the same, the essays offer some significant arguments. First, Bankim refutes colonialist ascriptions about the Hindu's 'effeminacy' by citing how the Hindu sepoy had won many a battle for the British and the brave resistance put up for a long time by the Sikhs and Marathas. India had, therefore, been subjugated not because Indians were weak or powerless but because they lacked a record of their previous military exploits that could have been the source of self-confidence and a new pride of race. In the case of Hindus, this was particularly galling as all histories related to them had been authored by non-Hindus. What the victors wrote about the vanquished, Bankim was quick to point out, was hardly likely to be objective or free from bias.

It was equally facile to argue, Bankim suggested, that Indians were not a freedom-loving people or that political subjection for them had become a matter of habit. This was clearly belied by the instance of Mewar that so valiantly fought the Mughals. The real problem, in Bankim's perception, was the mental constitution of the Hindu who showed a greater inclination towards mastering his self than his external environment. That apart, there was the discord and disunity natural to a civilization that had hosted such a great variety of races, cultures, religions, and linguistic groups. Under the circumstances, *jati pratistha*, an inner concordance between various peoples, communities, or races could not be established in pre-British India. The other important point that he makes is that foreign rule per se was not bad; it became oppressive and irresponsible when the sovereign himself was located in a different land and not sufficiently aware of the state of his subjects. A people truly lost their freedom when their legitimate demands could not be met.

In the essays specifically addressed to the problems in Bengal, Bankim advances two kinds of arguments. At one level, there is the reaffirmation of points more generally made in respect of India. Thus in the essay, '*Banglar Itihas*' ('The History of Bengal'), he reiterates his disappointment at the Hindus neglecting their own history. In Bankim's understanding, this grew out of the belief that man himself had no agency or power to effect social changes in this world. His short-lived and meaningless actions were, therefore, not worth commemorating. However, the more distinctive quality about these essays is the painstaking effort to recover the social and historical antecedents of Bengali Hindus. Occasionally, this leads Bankim to make exaggerated claims about what that community might have historically achieved. Thus, one hears of how Lakshman Sen (of the Sen dynasty) virtually ruled over one-third of Indian territory and of Bengalis being unsurpassed as colonizers in south and south-east Asia. Having praised his people so highly, it naturally became difficult for Bankim Chandra to accept current legends and beliefs about Bengal capitulating before just seventeen horsemen led by Bakhtiyar Khalji. He calls this historical fabrication in the hands of official chroniclers like Minhaj-us-Siraj in his *Tabaqat-i-Nasiri*. Here, Bankim's rections had to be largely personal for the work was still not available in any standard English translation. On the other hand, what his Muslim contemporaries may have reasonably objected to is the insinuation that one who was not Hindu in his acts or beliefs could not be trusted to be truthful in narrating the history of the Hindus. In his '*Banglar Itihas Sombondhe Koyekti Kotha*' ('A Few Words on the History of Bengal') he disputes the veracity of Minhaj's testimony, not on account of some professional failing but the fact that he was a 'cow-slaying, shaven-head Muslim'.

Interestingly enough, Bankim Chandra favourably contrasted Pathan rule over Bengal to that of the Mughals. Under the Pathans, Hindu Bengal had not lost her identity or independence as there still flowered a brilliant intellectual and cultural life. At the time, Bengal excelled as logicians (*nyayaiks*) and the great Vaishnava revival under Chaitanya occurred during the reign of Sultan Hussain Shah. On the other hand, Emperor Akbar, whom everyone acclaimed, was the man responsible for turning Bengal into a barren land, a mere shadow of her former self. The Mughals systematically siphoned off the resources of the province to build aesthetically pleasing monuments like the Taj Mahal. Hereafter, all that the Bengali heard of was *Jama* and *Asal*, relentless mechanisms of revenue extraction that, sadly, had been devised by a Hindu (Todar Mal).

Bankim Chandra wholeheartedly shared the view, well established in bhadralok society by his time, of the British rescuing

Bengal (and India) from the disorder that was the result of several centuries of Muslim rule. In 1857, when many parts of north India were rocked by anti-British uprisings, Bankim, then a law student at Presidency College, reportedly told his teacher (W.A. Montriou) that if for a moment the thought of the British losing India had crossed his mind, he would have promptly thrown his books into the Ganga and returned home. As a civil servant, he always remained apprehensive of arousing official suspicion. In a letter of January 1873, addressed to his friend Shambhu Chandra Mookerjee, Bankim showed great reluctance in publishing his 'The Confessions of a Young Bengal' in *Mookerjee's Magazine*. This is surprising to say the least, for, in this piece, the author took good care to publicise his 'high English education', a 'thoroughly English culture', and above all, the desire to 'reconstruct society according to English notions'. In the 1870s, he accused the Indian press of unnecessarily creating a general feeling of distrust towards the government. This annoyed popular papers like the *Amrit Bazar Patrika*. 'In a free country, such remarks from a person of Bankim Babu's position would have brought down upon him universal condemnation', the *Patrika* complained, 'but under the pressure of a foreign government, even the truest patriot turns a traitor to his country'. In Bankim's defence it might be said that his fears and extra caution seem vindicated by the Bengal government's charging him with 'seditious' intentions in *Anandamath*. Disciplinary action on similar grounds had also been instituted against some contemporary Bengali writers. A Brahmo *munsif*, Chandicharan Sen (1845–1906) was denied promotion for producing historical novels like *Maharaj Nand Kumar* (1885), *Ayodhyar Begum* ('The Begums of Awadh', 1886), and *Jhansir Rani* ('The Rani of Jhansi', 1888).

It was never Bankim's intention that rightful demands made by Indians be stifled every time by the administration; on the other hand, there is some reason to believe that he disapproved of both rushing to launch a political revolution as well as the methods currently adopted to bring this about. On the whole, Bankim believed that the time was not opportune for unleashing a long or violent resistance against the British and here, no doubt, he would have been reminded of the several infirmities or failings in personal character that he took Indians to suffer from. In *Anandamath* itself, as we may recall, the heroic Santans are ultimately persuaded by the Physician to lay down their arms before the British on the practical plea that they were not yet capable or suitably equipped to establish an independent Hindu kingdom. Freedom had therefore to wait until the time knowledge and power in Indians had not reached a level comparable to that of the British. Such thoughts, one must remember, are not apologetic backtracking but consistent with those expressed even in the 1870s. A healthy rivalry that an Indian might reveal before the Englishmen, Bankim argued, would only contribute to the development of his race. And emulation of one people by another was never in itself bad. After all, the good Englishman too, that the Bengali was now trying to emulate, had been brought up in the intellectual and cultural legacy of the ancient Greeks.

A radical change in the status quo obviously did not appeal to Bankim, partly because in this he feared the possibility of liberty being misread as licence. In the novel *Devi Chaudhurani*, the once rebellious Devi (Prafulla) warns rebel soldiers not to take the law into their own hands and her companion, Bhavani Pathak, like Satyananda in the *Anandamath,* retreats in the face of the belief that the country was now well administered by the British. A couple of years later, on the eve of Lord Ripon's departure for England, Bankim repeated the warning to the educated community, advising them not to unduly hasten a social and political revolution. A word in praise of the English was not necessarily a way to please one's superior or the cowardice of the faint-hearted. In Bankim's perception, Indian patriotism was not inconsistent with giving the British their due. His major complaint though was that even after ruling the country for over a hundred years, the Englishman really had no clue as to the true character of either India or Indians. There was no reason why loyal Indians could not be trusted to carry arms or be given positions in the government befitting their talent and status. Sadly again, India was being unjustly made to pay for Britain's wars and Home Charges were being levied year after year, exclusively to Britain's advantage.

On the state of contemporary politics, Bankim appears to have been sceptical. For one, it seemed to him to be far too taken up by the petty interests of the Babu. It was unduly adulatory of the English, far too mendicant in its demands, and wrongly given to believe that there was little beyond laying claim to seats in the city corporations or powerless legislative councils. In his *Ingrazstrotra* ('Hymns in Praise of an Englishman', 1872) the following is what he has an Indian plead before the Englishman:

> O Great One! Grant me wealth, grant me fame; please fulfil all my desires! Give me a good job, make me a Raja, a Raibahadur or at least a member of the Council. ... If somehow you do not wish to favour me with such rewards, do not forget to invite me to dinner at the outhouse or recommend my name on important Committees. ... Do make me a Justice, a Honorary Magistrate or a member of the Senate ... O Great one I bow down to you ! ... O Great one, after you listen to my speeches and read my essay, shower all your praise on me. This will enable me to bravely confront every criticism from Hindu society ... O Great One, I bow down to you!
>
> (Translated)

Admittedly, there are no clear suggestions by Bankim Chandra about broadening the social base of Indian nationalism or a turn towards greater political militancy. At the same time, for a whole generation of politicians after him, the cultural symbolisms that he had brought to use contributed considerably to the realization of such tasks.

## The Nation made Divine

While Bankim may have more evocatively expressed the same, the mystique of one's land of birth as the 'Mother' with divine attributes lies buried in far older Hindu philosophical concepts and imagery. In classical Indian literature, analogies had been commonly drawn between the procreative woman and fertile, bountiful nature. There are even glimpses of a 'Bharat Mata' in Sanskrit texts going back to the fifth–sixth century C.E. In the Hindu philosophical school of Sankhya, the term *prakriti* represented both a Creatrix and created nature. However, specifically in our context, it is important to recall that medieval

Bengal, together with neighbouring Orissa and Assam, was an important centre of the Sakta cult. The term Sakta stands for the votary of *Sakti*, an energising virility and power that was identified with the Goddess or Devi. Puranic mythology has it that it was only the Devi, assuming a variety of forms, who finally overpowered the mighty and indestructible *asura*s (demons) and thereby restored Righteousness and Order. In nineteenth century Bengal, this association of the Goddess with Power and as the last refuge of unhappy and emasculated men was clearly impregnated with new political and cultural meanings. For one, a clearer association now began to be made between a nurturing society and the motherly womb. Some years after Bankim Chandra, the militant political leader from Bengal, Bipin Chandra Pal (1858–1932), was to put this idea in the following words:

> Just as the foetus lives in the mother's womb, each of us is living in the womb of societal mother. Just as the mother's blood builds up the foetus, the mother's vitality protects the life of the child in the womb and gives it strength, the strength of society is derived from the wealth, knowledge and religion becomes the vehicle for resting place for each of us and lends greater justification to our individual existence.

Prior to Bankim, the reference to one's place of birth as the Mother occurs in at least two poems of Madhusudan Dutt—*Banga Bhumir Proti* ('An Ode to the Land of Bengal') and *Birbahu Kavya* ('The Saga of Birbahu'), published in 1862 and 1864, respectively. That such imageries became more political in their intentions is borne out by the sharp reactions of the Bengal Government to the poet Hemchandra Bandopadhyay's poem *Bharat Sangit* ('The Song of India', 1870). In Bankim Chandra himself, we first catch sight of such imagery in the essay '*Amar Durgotsav*' ('My Celebrations of the Durga Puja Festival') that was serialized in the *Bangadarshan* (October–November 1874) as a part of the collection of satirical essays, *Kamala Kanter Daptar*. Under the influence of opium, to which he is quite addicted, Kamala Kanta has the following vision of the Mother as described in his own words:

> I saw: suddently the stream of time surging towards and pervading the horizon ... I saw that stream in that endless, boundless, darkness, wave-tossed, and tempestuous ... I was utterly alone, and being alone began to

feel afraid, so alone without a mother 'Mother!, Mother!, I kept calling out ... Where, Oh where could my mother be? Where was the land of Bengal which that given birth to Kamala Kanta?

... Suddenly, heavenly music filled my ears, there in the horizon, like the rising of the morning sun, was the radiance of crimson glow. I felt a calming, gentle breeze and saw in the distance on that mass of heaving water, clad in gold, this ... image of Durga ... Was this my Mother? Yes, it was she! I knew her for my mother, the land of my birth, made of earth, in the form of clay, adorned with endless gems, now hidden in the womb of time. They were adorned with various powers in the form of different weapons, the enemy crushed at her feet ...

I cried out ... 'Protectress of your family and countless children Bestower of virtue, wealth, Happiness and sorrow! Accept my offering of flowers ... Come Mother, suffused with new Love, bearer of new strength, bold with new pride, beholding new dreams. Come Mother, enter our homes. ... Give your children power, giver of boundless power. ... We sixty million heads will throw ourselves at your feet ... Come, Mother, enter our homes. For she who has sixty million children need not fear ...'

But as I watched, I saw her no more, for that image sank in the boundless ocean of time ... Then with folded hands and tearful eyes, I cried out 'Rise again, Mother, golden land of Bengal! Mother, rise again. We will be good children now and tread the right path. We will protect your honour ... We will forget ourselves and love one another ...'

(Translation by Julius J. Lipner)

Here the opium addict, Kamala Kanta, is indeed Bankim's alter ego and three points emanating out of the above passage are especially worth noting. In the first place, we may wonder why the vision of the Goddess belongs to the surreal. Was this Bankim's way of complaining that the potent identification of the land of Bengal with the Mother was not yet sufficiently established in the minds of his people? Secondly, and quite paradoxically, the invocation reveals as much a protective deity as a deity that needs to be protected. While, on the one hand, the Mother extends to her numerous santans her ungrudging and benign protection, she, in turn, has to be reassured of support from her children. Perhaps a plausible explanation here is again Bankim's remaining circumspect about patriotic sentiments in fellow Bengalis. Understandably, there is, in this passage, not only an exhortation to patriotic duty but also the added emphasis on selflessness that Bankim was to fully develop both in his novels and treatises of the 1880s. A third and an apparently intriguing aspect to the passage is Bankim's allusion to 'sixty million santans'. Now by 1874, when the aforesaid essay appeared, the population of (Greater) Bengal must have been public knowledge for, the official Census Report had been published a good two years earlier. And yet, in the song 'Vande Mataram', to which we shall refer in more detail shortly and which is taken to have been composed around the same time, he puts the figure at seven crores (70 million). In 1872, the population of the territory administered by the Lt. Governor of Bengal (not including the princely states) was officially stated to be 60,502,897 which is certainly closer to sixty million than to seventy. The increase by 10 million in Bankim's estimates could be a laxness with figures; alternatively, it may well be that 'Vande Mataram' was composed closer to the 1880s than to the 1870s.

In *Anandamath*, importantly, Bankim reveals to us the motherland iconized as the Mother over three successive stages. This occurs in Part I, Chapter 11 of the novel when the rebel leader, Satyananda, leads the newly initiated Santan, Mahendra, into a series of secret chambers, entirely hidden from public view. Evidently, the underlying idea here is that all but the fully initiated are denied access to the secrets that are buried in these chambers. Here it would be important to remember that Satyananda uses the word 'santan' in a dual sense. On the one hand, there are those santans who are simply the children of the Mother in a general sense and who may remain ordinary householders. On the other, there are those that are fully converted to a cause. For the latter, initiation means not so much induction into a spiritual community as the willingness to forsake all thoughts of the self and family so that one may fully dedicate one's life to serving the motherland. It is true that men like Mahendra are drawn from the class of *grihastha*s (householders) and for a time, reveal the infirmity or weaknesses that such men develop in worldly life. But these are precisely the shortcomings that they also seek to conquer. The dharma of the intitiated Santan was service to the motherland, not moral obligations to his family and a closer scrutiny of the novel will reveal that in this case, even the women and wives help the men in the conquest of the self and in abiding by the vow that they have voluntarily undertaken. This is precisely the transformation that one finds in the couple, Mahendra and Kalyani.

In the sequence that we have referred to, Mahendra is first taken before the icon of the nurturing Mother Goddess, representing the motherland. This, importantly, is the Mother-as-she-was. Located in a still deeper and darker chamber is the Mother-as-she-is, in this instance, the dark and forbidding Goddess Kali. 'She, Kali, has been robbed of everything and that is why she is naked', Satyananda explains to a fearful Mahendra, 'And because (now) the whole land is a burning ground, she is garlanded with skulls'. This, we must note, is a deliberate inversion of the commonly accepted myth about the goddesss. In both Puranic mythology and folk imagination, Kali was never the benign, domesticated Goddess that Durga was and her nakedness was but a metaphor for a transitory world. The association of this Goddess with death and devastation, therefore, could not have been without a political intention. However, at the end of it all, there is also a redeeming vision. The Mother as she-will-be in the time to come is the resplendent, ten-armed Goddess, Durga, that Bengali folk culture had come to fondly regard as a daughter who returned every year to her parental abode on earth. It was to celebrate this home-coming that Bengal hosted the autumnal Durga Puja, a celebration that had as much an emotionally charged side as the social or ritual. It is hence with an emotionally choked voice that Satyananda describes this magnificent icon, her ten arms reaching out in the ten directions, the enemy lying fully humbled at her feet. In a fitting finale to this sequence, Mahendra, by now ecstatic with joy, asks, 'When will we be able to see the Mother in this form?' To this Satyananda gravely answers, 'When all the Mother's children recognize her as the Mother, she will be gracious to us'.

Bankim's underlying intentions, both in his *Amar Durgotsav* and the episode from *Anandamath* reproduced above, are amply clear. For one, his 'Durgotsav' (Durga Puja festivities) is not so much about the ritual worship of a Goddess such as was already common in Bengali public life, as the construction of a cultural and political icon which may prove to be a rallying point for a community. It is the power behind Devi symbolism, the quest for energizing sakti that captivates Bankim more than anything else. Interestingly, one may also locate here a strategic change in cultural preferences. Why did Bankim Chandra, a Vaishnava in his religious persuasion, opt to deliberately play with sakta symbolism? Arguably, the Santans in the novel *Anandamath* are not Vaishnavas in the narrow sense. A possible answer to this would be that given the strong roots that Bengal Vaishnavism had in both non-violence and a highly emotional view of religion, this would have ill-fitted Bankim's political agenda. The Goddess Durga and Durga Puja were traditionally established icons and institutions that were by their very nature or function, community-oriented. They fostered a vibrant community life and enabled men and women to go beyond themselves, however, temporarily.

## 'Vande Mataram': Conflicting Perceptions on a Song

It has been aptly observed that while some writings remain trapped inside the pages of a book, others were found to come out of them and become a part of everyday life. Surely, the song 'Vande Mataram' belongs to the latter category. Especially after it was introduced into the novel *Anandamath* in 1881, it has progressively become an icon by which one's loyalty to the nation has often been tested. In the words of one contemporary, it 'gave speech to the dumb and courage to the faint-hearted'.

Historically, it has been often possible to detach this song from its base in the novel, if not also from its specific context. Gandhi first read *Anandamath* in translation in 1937 while he had been enthused by the song even 'as a lad'. In the 1880s, when the song first became publicly known, it did produce some excitement in the local press. One Harish Chandra Haldar, for example, was led to pictorially depict 'Mother India' in the Bengali periodical, *Balak* (1885). Perhaps the first public appeal to use the song more extensively was made by a noted scholar and writer, Yogendranath Vidyabhushan (1845–1904) in his *Life of Garibaldi* (1890). However, insofar as the popularity of the song is concerned, the swadeshi era in Bengal clearly marks a watershed. The cry of 'Vande Mataram' was widely used as a political slogan at the protest meeting held at the Calcutta Town Hall in October 1905. A collection of patriotic songs by the same name ran into five editions within the same year and in 1906, Bengali enthusiasts launched the paper *Bande Mataram*, soon to be associated with the revolutionary leader, Aurobindo. By this time, the song had been translated into several major Indian languages. Its first translation into English was by the Bengali philologist, Harinath De, for the newspaper *Indian Mirror* in 1905. However, a better-known translation is that by Aurobindo for the paper *Karmayogin* in 1909. It was sung (to great effect) twice at Congress sessions, the first time by Rabindranath Tagore in 1896 and subsequently by his niece, Sarala Debi Chaudhurani, in 1905.

The continuing mass appeal of the song may be gauged from the famous contemporary music composer A.R. Rehman's setting it to an entirely new musical score and its recurring use in various public campaigns. In recent times, it has also been involved in some public controversy following the attempt made by certain state governments to introduce its compulsory singing in state-run schools. On this issue, objections came from both non-Hindus as well as certain political parties that took this to be a deliberate fanning of 'Hindutva' sentiments. In a work published in 1997 (*Jinnah, Pakistan and the Islamic Identity*) the writer, Akbar Ahmad, found a direct causal link between sentiments expressed in *Anandamath* and the damges inflicted on the mosque at Ayodhya. Serious allegations raised against the song first occurred in the late 1930s and 1940s when M.A. Jinnah and the Muslim League lodged strong protests against the public singing of a song loaded with Hindu religious motifs and imageries. Historically, therefore, the song has contributed to unite the nation as also to divide it. 'Vande Mataram', paradoxically enough, has been the passionate call to free India from alien rule but also regrettably, the war cry of Hindu communal rioters.

There is reason to believe that Bankim Chandra himself would have been somewhat uncomfortable with either of these positions, especially when taken to their extreme forms. Reportedly, he had great faith in the potentiality of the song and prophesied that one day, it would be the new, electrifying mantra of patriotism. It is also apparent that by the closing years of his life, he was quite disappointed to find that the song had not sufficiently enthused his countrymen. 'Of what use is my writing *Anandamath* or even your attempting to understand its underlying message', he wrote with a heavy heart to a friend at Dacca, 'I see no future for a self-seeking and greatly disunited people such as the Bengali. Instead of the slogan "Vande Mataram"("I bow to thee Mother"), let us cry "Vande Udaram" ("Glory to the Belly").' At the same time, close friends like the civil servant, Romesh Chandra Dutt, later wondered if Bankim would have at all approved of the 'evil notoriety' that the song acquired during the anti-Partition agitation in Bengal (1905–08). That Bankim's conclusions in *Anandamath* were quite acceptable to a section of the Bengali middle classes is apparent from the reaction in the local press. *The Liberal* of 8 April 1882, for instance, had the following to say:

> The passage (spoken by the Physician in the concluding part of the novel exhorting Satyananda to give up his struggle) embodies the most recent and most enlightened views of the educated Hindus and happening as it does in a novel powerfully conceived and easily executed, it will influence the whole race for the good. The author's dictum we heartily accept as it is one which already forms the creed of English education.

Objections raised chiefly by Muslims focused on stanza three of the song where the motherland is explicitly identified with the Puranic Durga, the Goddess with ten arms who humbles mighty *asura*s. However, one cannot be sure if in this instance, Bankim was reverting to Hindu image worship. *Prima facie*, this is difficult to relate to a man, who, in the 1870s, was strongly iconoclastic towards Hindu religion and culture. On the other hand, it is just possible that he made a distinction between the hard, rational, and argumentative quality of prose with poetic licence. As a novelist, he is known to have deliberately strayed from fact or history. While the novel *Anandamath* was based on certain historical events, Bankim used the prerogative of a creative writer to effect changes in plot and character. A close comparison between the first and the fifth editions (1882 and 1892, respectively) will reveal several interesting discrepancies. For one, the conflict between the Santans and their adversaries is geographically relocated but more importantly, by the fifth edition, the former are no longer fighting the English as much as the Muslims. Finally, whether deliberately or otherwise, Bankim is even careless with basic historical facts.

Thus, at the time of the Sanyasi and Fakir rebellions, on which the novel is based, the ruler of Bengal was not Mir Jafar but his sons, Sarf-ud-Daulah and Mubarak-ud-Daulah.

The bilingual (Sanskrit and Bengali) nature of the song 'Vande Mataram' has intrigued many a scholar. Stylistically, it seems to have been modelled on the Sanskrit *vandana* but this is offset by the random insertion of modern Bengali. Could it be that in Bankim's opinion, the Bengali language could not match the sonorous quality of Sanskrit? Alternatively, did he use Sanskrit so as to reach out to a pan-Indian Hindu élite, across linguistic divides? Surely, a song composed entirely in a regional language might have been more difficult to adopt as a national song. Here, it would only be fair to add that 'Vande Mataram' had several Hindu detractors. Rabindranath Tagore's Brahmo monotheism made him somewhat uncomfortable with the Puranic imageries in the song. Jawaharlal Nehru complained that he could comprehend several words in the song only with the help of a dictionary, and Gandhi, in the face of persistent Muslim criticism, was forced to point out that the overarching message of the song was political, not religious.

There has been persistent debate on whether or not Bankim may be accused of exhibiting an anti-Muslim feeling. Some are prepared to argue that that he was rabidly communal and missed no opportunity to vilify the Muslim. At first sight, this would indeed appear to be the case. Barring a few occasions, Bankim Chandra does not seem to have weighed the political or cultural implications of what he chose to say on these subjects. A more politically sensitive figure might have at least shown greater restraint with language and attempted to tone down its capacity to offend public feelings. Thus, in the novel *Rajsingha*, Emperor Aurangzeb is shown to retreat from the presence of his Hindu adversary, Rajsingha, 'like a dog with its tail between its legs'. In *Anandamath* (Part II, Chapter 7), an angry Hindu mob threatens to demolish a mosque. But perhaps the most provocative description comes from his novel *Sitaram*, where a woman, Sree, assumes the role of the blood thirsty goddess Chandi, crying out in a shrill voice to the Hindus to exterminate the Muslims, 'the enemy of the gods, of man and of all Hindus'.

By 'Bangla'/Bengal, Bankim could not have meant ethnic Bengal for the figure that he cites (*sapta koti*/seven crores) refers to the combined population of present day West Bengal, Bangladesh, Bihar, Jharkhand, Orissa, and Assam. Quite significantly, the figure is also inclusive of the Muslims and the tribal population. Under the circumstances, Bankim's conception of the motherland is clearly in a state of inner tension. On the one hand, it could not be exclusively Hindu and Bengali for in it are included non-Hindus and areas where Bengali was not the first language. On the other hand, such a conception looks presumptuous in that it takes diverse ethnic, religious, or linguistic groups to be culturally mobilized by using symbols or imageries specific to one group.

It is not surprising that such portrayals provoked angry Muslim responses. A prominent Muslim-owned daily, *Mihir-o-Sudhakar*, objected to the dramatization of the already contentious *Rajsingha* and one Gholam Hossain, in his *Bangla Deshiya Hindu-Mussalman* ('The Hindus and Muslims of Bengal', 1910) wrote bitterly how 'on every page of his (Bankim's) novels, the one prominent feature was directing invectives against the Muslim community as a whole'. By the 1920s, certain Muslim writers had begun to even parody Bankim Chandra and his novels in what would appear to be vicious, personalized attacks. A fairly well-known collection of such parodies appears in Abul Hossain's *Jnan Bhandar* (1924) in which Hindu domestic life is shown as being scandalized by gross immorality. A work of a similar nature was Sheikh Mohammad Idris Ali's *Bankim Duhita* (date not known). Referring to this work, the Bengali novelist, Sarat Chandra Chatterjee (1876–1938) remarked:

> A lot of dirty accusations are levelled in this novel but perhaps this is quite natural. Bankim Babu himself is known to have wantonly attacked the Muslims at several places. At the time, they (the Muslims) were a fairly docile community. However, every action is bound to have a reaction.

In the epilogue to a revised version of *Rajsingha,* Bankim denied any intentions of deliberately hurting Muslim sentiments. It was not the religious identity of a man that by itself made a man good or bad, he added. Aurangzeb, in this analysis, was humbled because of his failure to discharge the duties (dharma) of a monarch and

Rajsingha, the Rajput warrior, emerged victorious only because his conduct had all along been dharmic (virtuous). In the same novel, Bankim took care to show how a misguided Hindu too could be just as cruel and unjust towards other people as the Muslims had been shown to be. Thus, there is the instance of a Hindu official, Dayal Shah, who seeks retribution against Muslims by wantonly punishing Kazis and Muslim holy men and ordering copies of the Koran to be thrown into wells. At one level, Bankim may indeed have tried to separate the virtuous from the wicked rather than the Hindu from the Muslim. At quite another, there is no escaping the fact that whether rightly or wrongly, Bankim and men of his class and generation openly exhibited the feeling of being repeatedly wronged and oppressed under Indo-Muslim rule. Bankim himself shows great concern (on the basis of the 1872 Census) over a substantial percentage of Bengalis being Muslim. In a few years, this anxiety was to change into fears about Muslims outnumbering Hindus in Bengal.

That Bankim's portrayal of the Muslim was not more vigorously contested in his own province and at least not in his lifetime, may be explained with reference to the perceptibly different strengths and status of the Bengali Muslim in comparison to his counterpart from north India. Contestations between Hindu and Muslim élites were sharper in north India where their relative socio-economic standing was not as disparate as in Bengal. Besides, members of the Muslim aristocracy in Bengal that included names like Abdul Latif and Syed Amir Ali, were not particularly keen to assert their Bengali identity. This only made it easier for Bankim to deliberately gloss over the distinction between the Bengali Hindu and the Bengali Muslim.

Not every Muslim author or intellectual faulted Bankim for his unkind portrayal of the Muslim. A well-known Muslim writer, Rezaul Karim, dared to suggest that even Bankim's anti-Muslim bias would not really take away from his creative talent as a novelist. On the whole, Karim was unhappy at the way literary creations were used for political gain by both Hindus and Muslims. While he had the grace, the courage, and good sense to say that, not many after him have followed his example.

# 6

# The Last Years

MASTER: Man will turn God the day European science and technology unites with the spiritual self-control of India. Thereafter, such science and technology will be put to more positive use.
PUPIL: Will man ever see such a day?
MASTER: Why certainly! You Indians are eminently suited to bring about this synthesis. It is all in your hands. If you so desire, you could be the masters and leaders of the world. However, if you do not entertain such hopes, all this talking has been in vain.

—Bankim Chandra Chattopadhyay
(Translated from *Dharmatattwa*)

What is it for which we worship the name of Bankim today? What was his message to us or what the vision which he saw and helped us to see? He was a great poet, a master of beautiful language and a creator of fair and precious dream figures in the world of imagination; but it is as not a poet and stylist or novelist that Bengal does honour him today. ... It is the Bankim of the (later) works and not the Bankim of the great creative masterpieces who will rank among the Makers of Modern India. The earlier Bankim was only a poet and stylist, the latter a seer and nation-builder.

—Sri Aurobindo (1907)

In 1891, Bankim Chandra sought premature retirement from government service, partly on medical grounds but also so that he could spend more time on his various literary pursuits. At the time, this must have looked viable for a good number of Bankim's novels had indeed been conceived and even substantially completed while he was on medical leave from time to time. As it turned out, the last three years of his life were not very productive.

The government, however, readily acceded to his request and allowed him to retire (with effect from 14 September 1891) as Deputy Magistrate and Deputy Collector (Class I) at Alipore. In January 1892, it conferred on him the title of Raibahadur and exactly two years later, in 1894, with the C.I.E. between 1892 and 1894, Bankim completed short literary assignments that he was entrusted with. At the request of the University of Calcutta, he put together an anthology of Bengali literature (*Bengali Selections*) for use by examinees to the Entrance test conducted by that University. This was followed by a short introduction to the *Collected Works of Peary Chand Mitra* (who often wrote under the pseudomym, Tekchand Thakur) and of his elder brother, Sanjib Chandra. His last public appearances were in February–March 1894 when he delivered a series of lectures before the University Institute on the subject of Vedic literature.

Evidently, the major reason for Bankim Chandra not being able to fulfil the several tasks that he might have set for himself after retirement was his persistent ill-health. He had indeed suffered several afflictions and for long. That caused acute anxiety and depression as is evident from a letter he had written to Sanjib Chandra as early as 1874.

> Please do not be upset with me. I do not sufficiently trust my own body. It has been afflicted by many ailments, some quite serious. I do not seek cures for them since I have no desire to live long. A long life only means greater personal suffering and trouble even in seeking suitable remedies …
>
> (Translated)

A scrutiny of records pertaining to his official career reveals long periods of absence on medical grounds. During the period 1885–8, for instance, he was forced to take medical leave after asthmatic attacks. On 5 April 1894, he went into diabetic coma, but briefly regained consciousness only to pass away three days later on

8 April. The last rites were performed by his oldest nephew, son of Shyama Charan.

His wife, Rajlakshmi Debi, survived him by several years.

* * *

In 1873, Bengal lost two of her famous sons in Deenabandhu Mitra and Madhusudan Dutt, and Bengali literary life would have been considerably poorer in the next twenty years but for Bankim Chandra's prodigious contributions. In 1872, when Bankim launched the *Bangadarshan*, Rabindranath was only an adolescent and the next crop of Bengali literary 'greats' was yet to bloom. From the mid-1870s to the mid-1990s, it was Bankim Chandra who gave expression to the creative urges of the Bengali middle classes, to their cultural nostalgia, and perhaps more importantly, to their attempt to come to terms with a rapidly changing world.

Looking back at those years it appears as though this was carried out in two ways. First, there was the birth of a perceptibly new language and literature, which in turn, became vehicles for the dissemination of a new knowledge, a new way of conducting daily lives, a different way of looking at things. The effect that the *Bangadarshan* had on the contemporary Bengali mind has sometimes been compared to the effect that the French Encyclopedists had on revolutionary France. Such comparisons err on the side of exaggeration but even allowing for this, it would have to be said that new literary sensibilities and a serious engagement with contemporary international developments were indeed created at the time. Bankim Chandra's words not only breathed new life into a literary form that had not seen significant growth during the immediately preceding years but also created characters that Bengali readers had not known. They uninhibitedly reveal the compelling power of physical beauty and romance. They speak of the sublimating qualities of love as also of its socially perilous side, and even when the overwhelming mutual attraction between a man and a woman ends in tragic circumstances, one cannot but be touched by its tangible qualities. Notwithstanding his conservatism, Bankim remains etched in our memory as the supreme artiste whose creations seem to express or echo our deepest sentiments.

The other reason why Bankim represents such a key figure in colonial Bengal, and by extension in colonial India, is the way he sought to negotiate both modernity and tradition. More than any other Bengali of his generation, Bankim Chandra felt an acute need to historicize the intellectual and cultural profile of his people for only thus could he establish them in history. He chose to secure this in two ways. In the first place, there was the attempt to relate India's present to the past, to understand the contemporary state of Indian society and politics in the light of historical antecedents. Was it true, Bankim often asked himself, that Indians had been an intellectually feeble race and with whom a life of subjection had come to be habitually accepted? On such questions evidently, the past experiences of the people had to be taken as the vital key to understanding the present. On the other hand, this past could not be perceived entirely in its own terms for that would be perilously close to obscurantism. Rather, it had to be investigated through the use of analytical tools that were different from the ones traditionally used. The past, in other words, could at best be carefully adapted, not thoughtlessly adopted to contemporary social or intellectual needs. Social divisions had historically been common to all societies and across time, argued Bankim, but the basis on which they could now be established had to be significantly different from those in vogue earlier. Thus, a class or community had now to be defined not on the basis of some ascribed qualities, but that of the acquired. This was the way in which social leadership would have to be determined. In Bankim's understanding, one of the important changes that the modern world had seen was the perceptible shift in emphasis from an aristocracy of wealth to an aristocracy of talent. Knowledge and learning were now to be the basis of power, not inherited wealth or traditionally respected status. In his writings, Bankim Chandra took care to emphasize how men such as he belonged to the former.

Bankim's critical apparatus borrowed copiously and constructively from both the Western intellectual tradition and the Indian. Importantly, he used these not merely to critique one another but also to subject these to a deeper internal scrutiny. Hindu idolatry, for example, could be questioned both from the perspective of modern rationality borrowed from the West and also wisdom buried within the older Hindu tradition. This evidently fulfilled an important cultural need, for, to judge a far older civilization exclusively in terms of the modern weakened the general thesis that the purity and authenticity of a civilization were directly proportional to their historical age. The social and cultural practices of the past could be judged by applying the modern criteria of reason and utility; on the other hand, one could not be absolutely sure if these were at all modern.

Bankim often suggested that the substance of Western social theory, if not also its exact form, had long been anticipated by the Hindus. This, he suggested, was certainly true of Positivist thought though in their current state of social existence, this would not be so apparent in modern Hindus. At the same time, Bankim seems to have been only too aware of the practical limitations of an inter-cultural dialogue. It could be that here, he was questioning the universalistic pretensions of Enlightenment. Bankim clearly believed that every culture developed its own idioms of understanding and cross-cultural exchanges often erred in not displaying an adequate empathy or patience in deciphering meanings. Humanity had much in common; it was equally true, that specificities co-existed with shared cultural traits. Bankim evidently lamented the Indian habit of relying too much on European judgements even when these could be shown to be entirely in the wrong. He was equally uncomfortable with those among his co-religionists who believed that applying scientific phenomena to Hinduism would be more consistent with current intellectual fashions and hence more acceptable. He disliked Brahmo reformism because of its sectarianism; Hinduism, when suitably reformed, could be both universal and inclusive. Here, Bankim's thoughts clearly resonate with what Rammohun had already claimed before him and what Vivekananda was to claim later. On the whole, however, he was more critical of the European's masquerading as the expert on Hindu religion and culture than of misguided Hindus who were thoughtlessly trying to emulate the West. There is a powerful streak of counter-Orientalism in Bankim that openly questioned European verdicts on India and Indians. Max Mueller he thought to be patently wrong in his interpretations but a greater challenge, as one can see, is thrown at critics like Hastie. In 1882, Bankim wondered if men such as him at all possessed the qualifications (*adhikar*) to debate with a Brahman such as himself on the subject of Hinduism. In his debates with Evangelists too, Bankim contested the common association of monotheistic religion with greater sophistication in culture. The evidence he mustered in support of his arguments were drawn from non-Indian cultures. The culturally sophisticated Greeks, he argued, worshipped many gods and goddesses while the Jews, who were strict monotheists, could hardly lay claim to great cultural accomplishments.

The historicism of Bankim Chandra led him to conclude that all that was associated with Hinduism did not necessarily constitute it. In a sense, this was but a reiteration of an older critique, first developed by Rammohun, that a rationally tenable and a spiritually elevating religion of the Hindus had been steadily corrupted over time. Any meaningful attempt to restore it would, therefore, imply surgically removing a lot of the 'rubbish' that had accumulated over time. Bankim often tried to assess the religious or cultural life of a people by asking whether or not these rested on socially useful practices. On this, he was occasionally driven to extremes. In Bankim's judgement, rather than concede that what had been traditionally accepted in religious life could be proved useful, it had to assume that what was useful alone qualified to be counted as true religious life. This was the substance of his argument made in the 1890s on the question of whether or not sea travel could be undertaken by Hindus without being declared outcastes. Here, Bankim argued that since such travel had proved beneficial to the Hindus, it had to assumed to be a part of 'authentic' Hinduism. Especially coming from Bankim, and in the 1890s, this Utilitarian view of religion or religious life seems somewhat surprising. Ten years earlier, Bankim had declined to reprint the *Samya* on the ground that the impact that Mill and the Utilitarians had once made on his mind had been substantively blown away. For the author of *Dharmatattwa*, mere utility could not bring about a joining of hearts and the affinity that one man may feel with another. *Manusye preeti*, an expansive love of humanity as a whole, was thus a better ideal than 'the greatest good of the greatest number'. However, what Bankim could not convey as clearly as did Vivekananda after him was that there was not only a social side to man but also a spiritual one.

A problem of a different order occurs with Bankim's identification of 'authentic' Hinduism. It was his recurring argument that older thought and practice had to be suitably re-interpreted in the light of contemporary requirements. But in so arguing, Bankim also seems to exhaust his interpretative project. Why is it that modern Hinduism had to ultimately seek the mandate of the past? To put it more concretely, why did Bankim believe that suitably re-interpreting a classic text like the Bhagavad Gita was more meaningful than creating an altogether new compendium of modern religious thought? And was it possible that a certain tradition could have its most vital meaning stretched interminably? Apparently, Bankim never paused to address these critical questions. A community trying to critically redefine its place in a rapidly changing world, one imagines, would be under some constraint to create something synthetic and new besides adapting the old to changing needs or demands. In the religious history of modern Bengal, this is where the work of Bankim substantially differed from that of Maharshi Debendranath Tagore and the Brahmo Samaj. The latter gave vent to their dissatisfaction with tradition by creating a new source-book for themselves, the *Brahmodharmagrantha*, rather than merely re-interpreting the old. Bankim's position, by contrast, would appear to be more ambivalent. On the one hand, he takes a dynamic view of tradition by suggesting that it ought to be continuously re-interpreted; on the other, he appears to freeze tradition in time by suggesting that 'authentic' Hinduism may be located in a work like the Gita.

A more enduring legacy of Bankim was the discursive joining of older religious and philosophical paradigms to new political intentions. In *Dharmatattwa*, Bankim ran into some trouble over explaining how political work could be wholly devoid of expectations (nishkam). After all, what would a patriot look forward to if not the attainment of freedom? There was, at the time, an apocryphal story of the Bengali patriot who lost all interest in political agitations upon learning that freedom would not arrive in his lifetime. Bankim could do no more than hedge the issue by suggesting that political duty rendered to one country was indeed nishkam for here, the gains were not individual but affecting the whole community. Yet another way in which Bankim's writings proved useful to posterity was his using the categories of religion and politics interchangeably. What we have earlier called neo-Puranism, became an influential ideology especially after Bankim, and in the hands of men easily identifiable with militant, mass-based politics. In the context of Bengal, the three names that readily come to mind are those of Brahmabandhab Upadhyay (1861–1907), Aswini Kumar Dutta (1856–1923), and Bipin Chandra Pal (1858–1932), all of whom contributed substantially to a recasting of the Krishna legend and Krishna-bhakti. The idea of a God guiding the destinies of a nation and producing a bonding of hearts by His omnipresence is tacitly suggested in *Krishna Charitra*, but later acquired a more evocative form. In his famous Uttarpara speech (1909), Aurobindo referred to the divine visions that both he and his political co-worker, Bipin Chandra Pal, had while in a colonial jail:

> When Bipin Chandra Pal came out of jail, he came with a message and it was an inspired message. ... He spoke of his realization in jail of God within us all, of the Lord within the nation, and in his subsequent speeches also, he spoke of a greater than ordinary force in the movement and greater than ordinary purpose before it. That message which Bipin Chandra Pal received in Buxar jail, God gave to me in Alipore.

Again that which is only hinted at by Bankim became a powerful motif in both Vivekananda and Aurobindo. Collectively, they assert that the process of evolution had to have its counterpoint in what they call 'involution'. Life that evolved out of a higher Being would eventually return to it in due process. Hence, if God was to descend on earth as man, it was just as possible that man would one day ascend to godhood.

In *Dharmatattwa*, Bankim Chandra anticipated Vivekananda and many other Indian thinkers in constructing the stereotypes of a spiritually exalted India and a materially advanced West.

As a claim, this looked quite tendentious to even the unlettered saint, Sri Ramakrishna. Men in the West too could be spiritually gifted, the saint argued, and many Hindus, could be wicked. What this obviously overlooks is that in the hands of men like Bankim, the point about an enhanced spirituality too could be primarily political. The gift of a spiritual life was the Hindu's way of re-establishing himself in an unequal world. It was a way of asserting that ancient civilizations like the Indian, even when weakened and corrupted over time, had still much to give to the world. Vivekananda put this very well when he quipped how (Indians) 'will not be students always but teachers also. There could not be any friendship without equality and no equality when one party was always the teacher'.

Posterity has tended to read Bankim Chandra in several ways—another way of saying that his life and work have appealed to various people for a variety of reasons. Such reasons, in many cases, have been related to history. Thus, visions of the nation as Mother might have been more opaque and cries of 'Vande Mataram' by political enthusiasts less vociferous had it not been for the radical turn in Indian politics following the partition of Bengal in 1905. In the two major political agitations launched by Indians in Bankim's own lifetime, one in support of the Ilbert Bill which proposed to empower an Indian jury to judge Europeans and the other against the contempt case instituted against the nationalist leader, Surendranath Banerjee (by a European Judge), neither of these had attained any measure of popularity. The projection of Bankim Chandra primarily as a sage and political prophet by Aurobindo is again an instance of political opportunism. It might even be said that here, Aurobindo was somewhat in error by implying that the later Bankim was a patriot while the earlier was not. A concern for *jati-sanhati* that might be broadly translated as the unity of the races, an enduring joining of hearts, is transparent in Bankim's writings even in the 1870s. One is indeed inclined to think that for him, patriotism was first a matter of feeling and only subsequently, of action. And certainly, he did not trust organized politics to succeed without a wider dissemination of the political will or empty agitation to be replaced by sincere political sentiments. Was this not what Bankim Chandra meant by the term 'non-political patriotism'?

The unity that Bankim Chandra visualized was more intra-racial in nature than an inter-racial one. Like many Hindu thinkers who followed him, Bankim often used the categories 'Hindu' and 'Indian' interchangeably. However, for better or worse, this is also how he chose to define his own identity. Many cultures and religions had been historically present in India, he once argued, without also substantially altering the essential identity of India. Islam and Christianity had, no doubt, affected the destinies of India and yet had no claim on her 'national' religion. In Bankim's perception, India was quintessentially Hindu. On the other hand, there is good reason to doubt if this 'Hinduness' is translatable as the far more tendentious 'Hindutva'.

# Appendix A
## Chronology of Events

| | |
|---|---|
| 1838 | Birth at Kanthalpara on 26 June. |
| 1844 | Admitted to the English School, Midnapore, studies there until 1848. |
| 1849 | Married to Mohini Debi, then five years old; enters Mohsin College, Hoogly. |
| 1852 | First poetic and prose compositions published in the paper *Sangbad Prabhakar.* |
| 1854–6 | Awarded Junior and Senior Scholarships; first work *Lalita O Manas* published; admitted to Law Section of Presidency College, Calcutta. |
| 1857 | Passes Entrance Examination to Calcutta University in the first division. |
| 1858 | Secures first place (in second division) in the first B.A. examination held by Calcutta University; studies Law in Presidency College until 7 August. On 6 August, is appointed to the position of Deputy Magistrate and Deputy Collector (Jessore) by order of Lt. Governor. Joins duty on 23 August. |
| 1859–60 | Death of Mohini Debi; marries Rajlakshmi Debi, then twelve years old. |
| 1864 | First novel *Rajmohan's Wife* serialized in *Indian Field*. |
| 1865 | Jadav Chandra denies Shyama Charan and Bankim Chandra of their share of the ancestral property; beginnings of dispute between brothers; first Bengali novel *Durgeshnandini* published. |
| 1869 | Passes Law Examination, secures third place in the first division. |
| 1870 | Death of mother. |
| 1872 | *Bangadarshan* launched at Bhawanipore, Calcutta. |
| 1874–5 | Criminal case instituted against Col. Duffin; first meeting with Rabindranath Tagore. |

| | |
|---|---|
| 1876 | *Bangadarshan* ceases publication; rights transferred to Sanjib Chandra; Bankim partly translates his novel *Bishbriksha* as *The Bane of Life,* later presented to Lady Elliott. |
| 1877 | Family disputes intensify; Bankim leaves Kanthalpara for a rented house at Chinsura; *Bangadarshan* resumes publication under the editorship of Sanjib Chandra. |
| 1878–9 | Serious literary debates and discussions at Chinsura involving Bhudeb Mukhopadhyay, Hem Chandra Bandopadhyay, Jogendra Chandra Ghosh, and Pandit Ramgati Nyayratna. |
| 1880 | Begins writing *Anandamath.* |
| 1881 | Death of Jadav Chandra; differences with Magistrate Buckland at Howrah. |
| 1881–2 | Lives in a rented house at Bow Bazaar Street, Calcutta; draft copy of *Anandamath* read out before friends; resumption of literary meetings involving several prominent Bengali writers; discussion on Positivism with Jogendra Chandra Ghosh; visit to Tagore family residence at Jorasanko; controversy with Rev. Hastie; publication of *Anandamath.* |
| 1883 | Differences with Magistrate Westmacott; *Bangadarshan* closes down a second time; briefly revived but finally ceases publication in early 1884. |
| 1884 | Launches *Prochar* jointly with son-in-law, Rakhal Chandra Bandopadhyay; his last novel, *Sitaram* serialized in *Prochar;* differences with Adi Brahmo Samaj. |
| 1885–6 | Made member of Calcutta University Senate. |
| 1887 | Purchases house in Calcutta; proceeds on a pilgrimage to north India with brothers; felicitated at Khusrau Bag, Allahabad. |
| 14 Sept. 1891 | Retires from government service; settles down in Calcutta. |
| 1892 | Government confers title of Raibahadur on him. |
| 1894 | Government confers C.I.E.; lectures on 'Vedic Literature' at the University Institute, Calcutta; acute diabetic attack; dies on 8 April. |

# Appendix B
## Chronological List of Major Literary Works

*Novels*

| No. | Name of the novel | First appeared in | First published as book | Number of reprints in Bankim's lifetime | Other relevant details |
|---|---|---|---|---|---|
| 1. | *Rajmohun's Wife* (English) | *Indian Field* (1864) | 1935 | – | Bankim himself translated the first seven chapters into Bengali. |
| 2. | *Durgeshnandini* | – | 1865 | 13 times, last in 1893 | Translated into English as the *Chieftain's Daughter* by Charu Chandra Mookerjee, Calcutta, 1880; staged 11 times during 1873–5. |

| No. | Name of the novel | First appeared in | First published as book | Number of reprints in Bankim's lifetime | Other relevant details |
|---|---|---|---|---|---|
| 3. | *Kapala Kundala* | – | 1866 | 7 times, last in 1888 | Translated into English by Gopal Krishna Ghosh for the *National Magazine* (1876–7); by Debendra Nath Ghosh in 1919, H.A.D. Philips in 1885; staged 5 times during 1873–5. |
| 4. | *Mrinalini* | – | 1869 | 8 times, last in 1883 | Staged thrice during 1873–5. |
| 5. | *Bishbriksha* | *Bangadarshan* 1279 B.S. (1872–3) | 1873 | 8 times, last in 1892 | Translated into English by Miriam S. Knight as *The Poison Tree* (1884) partly translated by Bankim himself as *The Bane of Life* and gifted to Lady Charles Elliott; staged once during 1873–5. |
| 6. | *Indira* | *Bangadarshan* Chaitra 1279 B.S. (March–April 1873) | 1873 | 5 times, last in 1893 | Translated into English by J.D. Anderson as *Indira and Other Stories* (1919). |
| 7. | *Yugalanguriya* | *Bangadarshan* Baisakh 1280 B.S. (April–May 1873) | 1874 | 5 times, last in 1893 | Translated into English as *The Two Rings* by Rakhal Chandra Banerjee (1897); as *The Story of the Two Rings* |

| | | | | | |
|---|---|---|---|---|---|
| | | | | | (1913) by P.N. Bose and H.W.B. Moreno; and as *The Two Rings and Radharani* by D.C. Roy (1919). |
| 8. | *Chandrashekhar* | *Bangadarshan* 1280–1 BS (1873–4) | 1875 | 3 times, last in 1889 | Translated into English by Manmath Nath Ray Chaudhury (1904) and by Debendra Chandra Mallik (1905). |
| 9. | *Radharani* | *Bangadarshan* 1282 BS (1875) | 1876 | 4 times, last in 1893 | Translated into English and included in *The Two Rings and Radharani* (1919) by D.C. Roy and by R.C. Mallik (1910). |
| 10. | *Rajani* | *Bangadarshan* 1281–82 BS (1874–5) | 1877 | 3 times, last in 1887 | Translated into English by P. Majumdar (1928). |
| 11. | *Krishna Kanter Will* | *Bangadarshan* 1282, 1284 BS (1876, 1877–8) | 1878 | 4 times, last in 1892 | Translated into English by Dakshina Charan Roy (1918). |
| 12. | *Rajsingha* | *Bangadarshan* 1284, 1285 BS (1878) | 1882 | 4 times, last in 1893 | The 1893 edition had 434 pages as against only 83 pages of the 1882 edition. |

| No. | Name of the novel | First appeared in | First published as book | Number of reprints in Bankim's lifetime | Other relevant details |
| --- | --- | --- | --- | --- | --- |
| 13. | *Anandamath* | *Bangadarshan* 1287–9 BS (1881–2) | 1882 | 5 times, last in 1892 | Translated by Naresh Chandra Sen Gupta as *The Abbey of Bliss* (1906); by Aurobindo and Barindra Kumar Ghose for *Karmayogin* (1909–10); by Basanta Koomar Roy as *Dawn Over India* (1941), re-published with the original Bengali title in 1992; and by Julius J. Lipner as *Anandamath or The Sacred Brotherhood* (2005). |
| 14. | *Devi Chaudhurani* | *Bangadarshan* 1289–90 BS (1882–3) | 1884 | 6 times, last in 1891 | Bankim himself translated part of the novel into English; English translations (identity of translator unknown) were also published from Amritsar (1893) and Lucknow (1906). |
| 15. | *Sitaram* | *Prochar*, 1291 B.S., 1293 B.S (1884, 1887) with an intervening gap | 1887 | 3 times, last in 1894 shortly after Bankim's death | Partly translated into English as *Sree, an episode from Sitaram* by P.N. Bose and H.W.B. Moreno (1919). |

*Major Works of Non-Fiction (Bengali)*

| No. | Work | First appeared in | First published as book | Number of reprints in Bankim's lifetime | Other relevant details |
|---|---|---|---|---|---|
| 1. | *Lokrahasya* | *Bangadarshan* 1279–80 BS (1872–3) | 1874 | 2nd ed., 1888 | 2nd edition had 17 essays of which 8 were reprints from the first edition. |
| 2. | *Vigyan Rahasya* | *Bangadarshan* 1279–80 BS (1872–3) | 1875 | 2nd ed., 1884 | – |
| 3. | *Kamala Kanter Daptar* | *Bangadarshan* 1280–2 BS (1873–5) | 1875 | 2nd ed., 1885, reprinted 1891 | 2nd edition published as *Kamala Kanto* including two new works, *Kamala Kanter Potro* and *Kamala Kanter Jobanbondi.* |
| 4. | *Vividh Samalochana* | *Bangadarshan* (1873–5) | 1876 | – | Collection of select book reviews. Between 1873 and 1875, Bankim reviewed 11 books for the *Bangadarshan.* |

| No. | Work | First appeared in | First published as book | Number of reprints in Bankim's lifetime | Other relevant details |
|---|---|---|---|---|---|
| 5. | *Samya* | *Bangadarshan* 1279, 1280, 1282 BS (1872, 1873, 1875) | 1879 | – | Included essays by this name in the *Bangadarshan* and also *Bongodesher Krishak* from the same periodical. |
| 6. | *Probondho Pustak* | *Bangadarshan* 1279–81 BS (1872–4) | 1889 | – | Anthology of essays, later included in *Vividha Probondho.* |
| 7. | *Muchiram Guder Jeebon Charit* | *Bangadarshan* 1287 BS (1880) | 1884 | – | – |
| 8. | *Krishna Charitra —Prothom Bhag* (Part I) | *Prochar* 1291–3 BS (1884–6) | 1886 | 2nd ed. 1892 | Longest of Bankim's non-fiction works. |
| 9. | *Vividh Probondho —Prothom Bhag* (Part I) | *Bangadarshan* 1279-81 BS (1872–4) | 1887 | – | Anthology of essays including *Probondho Pustak* and *Vividh Samalochana.* |
| 10. | *Dharmatattwa —Prothom Bhag* (Part I) | *Nabajeebon* 1291 BS (excluding | 1888 | – | – |

| | | | | | |
|---|---|---|---|---|---|
| | | some numbers) (1884–5) | | | |
| 11. | *Vividh Probondho —Dwitio Bhag* (Part II) | *Prochar* 1291–2 BS; *Bangadarshan* 1282 BS (1875) | 1892 | – | Anthology of 22 essays. |
| 12. | *Srimad Bhagavatgita* (unfinished commentary on the Gita) | *Prochar* 1293, 1295 BS (1886, 1888–9) | 1902 | – | Posthumously published by Bankim's grandson putting together essays published in the *Prochar* and unpublished notes. |
| 13. | *Debtattwa O Hindu Dharma* | *Prochar* 1291–2 BS (1884–5) | After 1939 | – | Collection of essays first brought out in book form by Bangiya Sahitya Parishat under supervision of Sajani Kanto Das. |

*Major Works of Non-Fiction (English)*

| No. | Work | First appeared in | Other relevant details |
|---|---|---|---|
| 1. | 'On the Origin of Hindu Festivals' | Transactions of the Bengal Social Science Association, Vol. III, 1869 | Paper read before Bengal Social Science Association, 20 January 1869. |
| 2. | 'A Popular Literature for Bengal' | Transactions of the Bengal Social Science Association, Vol. IV, 1870 | Paper read before the Bengal Social Science Association, 28 February 1870. |
| 3. | 'Bengali Literature' | *Calcutta Review*, 1871, No. 104 | – |
| 4. | 'Buddhism and the Sankhya Philosophy' | *Calcutta Review*, 1871, No. 106 | – |
| 5. | 'The Confessions of a Young Bengal' | *Mookerjee's Magazine*, December 1872 | |
| 6. | 'The Study of Hindu Philosophy' | *Mookerjee's Magazine*, May 1873 | |
| 7. | Letters in the Hastie Controversy | *The Statesman*, 23 September 1882 to 22 November 1882 | 11 letters in all; 6 from Rev. W. Hastie, 4 from Bankim Chandra (psend: Ram Chandra) and one from Rev. K.M. Bandopadhyay. |

| | | | |
|---|---|---|---|
| 8. | Letters on Hinduism | Probably written between 1882 and 1887 | Found in manuscript form by Bimal Chandra Sinha of the Paikpara Raj family; written to a Positivist friend, Jogendra Chandra Ghosh of Kidderpore (Calcutta). |

# Suggested Readings

Note: This is a list of readings in the English language only.

Two early pieces by Sri Aurobindo, *Bankim Chandra Chatterjee* (originally published in *Indu Prakash*, 1894) and *Bankim-Tilak-Dayanand* (originally published in *Bande Mataram*, 1907) are now available as various reprints from Sri Aurobindo Ashram, Pondicherry.

The standard biography of Bankim in English is by Sisir Kumar Das (*The Artist in Chains: A Life of Bankim Chandra Chatterji*, New Delhi: New Statesman Publishing Company, 1984). An analysis of Bankim's social and political thought is available in B.B. Majumdar's *History of Indian Social and Political Thought: From Rammohun to Dayanand*, Calcutta: Firma K.L. Mukhopadhyay, 1967; Amalesh Tripathi's *The Extremist Challenge*, Calcutta: Orient Longman, 1967; and Tapan Raychaudhuri's *Europe Reconsidered: Perceptions of the West in Nineteenth Century Bengal*, New Delhi: Oxford University Press, 1988. A useful collection of essays on various aspects of Bankim Chandra's life and thought is available in Bhavatosh Chatterjee's edited volume, *Bankim Chandra Chatterjee: Essays in Perspective*, New Delhi: Sahitya Akademi, 1974.

Advanced works dealing with specific aspects of Bankim's thought, especially his reinterpretation of dharma are Rachel van Baumer's 'The Reinterpretation of Dharma in Nineteenth Century Bengal' in *Aspects of Bengali History and Society*, edited by Rachel van Baumer, Delhi: Vikas, 1975; Ursula King's 'True and Perfect Religion: Bankim Chandra's Reinterpretation of Hinduism,' in *Religion* 7 (1977); *Philology and Confrontation: Paul Hacker on Traditional and Modern Vedanta*, edited by W. Halbfass, Albany: State University of New York Press, 1965; and W. Halbfass's *India and Europe: An Essay in Understanding*, Albany: State University of New York Press, 1988.

A valuable though somewhat difficult work on Bankim's political thought is Sudipta Kaviraj's *The Unhappy Consciousness: Bankim Chandra Chattopadhya and the Formation of Nationalist Discourse in India*, New

Delhi: Oxford University Press, 1995; Jasodhara Bagchi's 'Representing Nationalism: Ideology of Motherhood in Colonial Bengal,' *Economic and Political Weekly* (October 20–7 1990) is an interesting and informative essay on the mother symbolism in *Anandamath*.

On Bankim and the Hindu–Muslim problem, see Amalesh Tripathi's *The Extremist Challenge* (cited above); T.W. Clark's 'The Role of Bankim Chandra in the Development of Nationalism' in *Historians of India, Pakistan and Ceylon*, edited by C.H. Philips, London: Oxford University Press, 1967; and Tanika Sarkar's 'Imagining Hindu Rashtra: The Hindu and Muslim in Bankim Chandra's Writings' in *Making India Hindu*, edited by David Ludden, New Delhi: Oxford University Press, 1996.

Some works of non-fiction by Bankim have been translated into English. Pradip Bhattacharya has translated the *Krishna Charitra* (see his *Krishna Charitra: Translated from the Bengali with an Introduction*, Classics of the East Series, Delhi, 1991).The *Dharmatattwa* has recently been translated by Apratim Ray and the edition includes a critical introduction by Amiya P. Sen (New Delhi: Oxford University Press, 2003). There is an excellent translation of Bankim's commentary on the Gita by Hans Harder (see *Bankim Chandra Chattopadhyay's Srimadbhagavatgita Translation and Analysis by Hans Harder*, Delhi: Manohar, 2004).

Some of Bankim's sociological essays like *Samya* are available in translation. For this, see M.K. Haldar's *Renaissance and Reaction in Nineteenth Century Bengal*, Calcutta: Minerva Press, 1977, and S.N. Mukherjee's *Bankim Chandra Chatterjee: Sociological Essays*, Calcutta: Rdhi India, 1986. Recent translations of Bankim's novels include Julius J. Lipner, (trans.), *Anandamath*, Oxford: Oxford University Press, 2005,